THE CHINESE IN AMERICA

The IN AMERICA *Series*

THE CHINESE IN AMERICA

CLAIRE JONES

Published by
Lerner Publications Company
Minneapolis, Minnesota

ACKNOWLEDGMENTS

The illustrations are reproduced through the courtesy of: p. 6, Trustees of the British Museum; p. 9, Museum of Fine Arts, Boston; pp. 12, 14, 80, The Peabody Museum of Salem; pp. 19, 21, United States Signal Corps, National Archives; p. 23, United States Information Agency, National Archives; p. 25, The White House; p. 28, Smithsonian Institution; p. 32, New York Public Library; p. 37, Thomas Gilcrease Institute, Tulsa, Oklahoma; p. 38, California State Library; pp. 41, 44, Independent Picture Service; pp. 48, 73, United Press International, Inc.; p. 50, Hawaiian Historical Society; p. 51, United States Office of War Information, National Archives; pp. 55, 57, 60, 75, California Historical Society; pp. 62, 69, Library of Congress; pp. 65, 66, San Francisco Chamber of Commerce; p. 79, Cherokee Book Shop; p. 82, Howard Wong's; p. 85, United States Senate Republican Policy Committee; p. 86, Tsai Management and Research Corporation; p. 88, Dong Kingman; p. 89, James Wong Howe; p. 90, I. M. Pei; p. 91, Tsung Dao Lee; p. 93, Columbia University, Office of Public Information.

LIBRARY OF CONGRESS CATALOGING IN PUBLICATION DATA

Jones, Claire.
   The Chinese in America.

   (The In America Series)
   SUMMARY: Discusses reasons for immigration of the Chinese to the United States, their problems here, and their contributions to American life.

   1. Chinese in the United States—Juvenile literature. [1. Chinese in the United States] I. Title.

E184.C5J6   917.3'06'951   72-3585
ISBN 0-8225-0223-2

International Standard Book Number: 0-8225-0223-2
Library of Congress Catalog Card Number: 72-3585

Second Printing 1974

...CONTENTS...

PART I.   Life behind the Great Wall of China

    1. *China's Ancient Culture* 7

    2. *East Meets West* 11

    3. *The Opium War* 15

    4. *Chinese Emigration in the 19th Century* 18

    5. *The Birth of Modern China* 20

PART II.   Land of the Golden Mountains

    1. *Early Settlers in California* 26

    2. *California Beckons to the Chinese* 28

    3. *In the Goldfields* 30

    4. *Building the Railroad* 33

    5. *"Not a Chinaman's Chance"* 37

PART III.   Restriction of Chinese Immigration

    1. *Discrimination Gets the Support of the Law* 43

    2. *Exclusion of Chinese Immigrants* 45

    3. *Repeal of the Exclusion Laws* 50

PART IV.   Chinatowns in America

    1. *Home Away from Home* 54

    2. *The Big City of the Golden Mountains* 59

    3. *The Earth Dragon Trembles* 62

    4. *Rebuilding in San Francisco* 63

    5. *Chinatowns in Other American Cities* 67

    6. *The Decline and Rise of American Chinatowns* 70

PART V.   Changing Attitudes toward Chinese Americans

    1. *Social, Political, and Economic Pressures* 74

    2. *Influence of Newspapers, Movies, and Books* 77

    3. *Chinoiserie in America* 80

PART VI.   Individual Achievements

    1. *Above-Average Jobs* 83

    2. *Government Officials* 85

    3. *Businessmen* 86

    4. *Artists and Craftsmen* 87

    5. *Research Scientists* 91

Index 94

This bronze wine vessel in the shape of two rams was used in religious rituals during the Shang dynasty. It is over 3,000 years old.

PART I

Life behind the Great Wall of China

1. *China's Ancient Culture*

When America was still the land of the Indian, and Columbus had not yet set out on his historic voyage, China could already look back on 3,200 years of history. Like Egypt and the Mesopotamian and Indus valleys, China was the scene of one of the earliest developments of human civilization.

From its beginnings, Chinese history has traditionally been divided into dynasties, periods during which different royal families held power. The ruling dynasty of Shang, dating from about 1770 to 1030 B.C., is the oldest that archeologists have yet been able to establish. Stories are told of earlier dynasties, but so far no one knows exactly where legend ends and history begins. Further investigation may yet prove that the legends are based on fact.

During the early Shang dynasty, a high level of civilization had already been achieved in China. A system of writing existed, and the use of bronze and of horse-drawn chariots was known. Today museums around the world display the beautiful art and craftsmanship of the Shang period—enormous bronze vessels used in religious rituals, elaborate bronze wine goblets, pieces of delicately carved jade.

The Shang dynasty was succeeded by the Chou dynasty, which ruled until 256 B.C. Confucius, that often misquoted scholar and philosopher, lived during this period, from about 551 to 479 B.C. Confucius was one of the world's earliest advocates of law and order. He and his followers believed that good government and a good society in general were based on the principles of order and duty. Each man, whatever his station in life, was bound by obedience to those above him and by responsibility to his inferiors. Even the Celestial Emperor, at the head of the earthly hierarchy, was obliged to honor and obey the gods. The many gods in heaven also had their own hierarchy and could be approached only through a man's dead ancestors.

After Confucius's death, the scholars who followed his teachings wrote books setting down an elaborate code of ethics and etiquette for the ruling classes. These books, which came to be known as the Confucian classics, were very influential in shaping Chinese culture and society. They provided a pattern of behavior for the aristocracy and eventually for the vast army of government officials (mandarins) who ran the Chinese empire until its collapse in the early 20th century.

China was first united by Chin Shih Huang Ti (221-210 B.C.), the first emperor of the Chin dynasty. Shih Huang Ti provided for the defense of his empire by building the Great Wall, a 1,500-mile barrier formed by joining many separate walls along China's northern border. The Great Wall sealed the Celestial Empire off from the nomad barbarians of the north.

During his reign, Shih Huang Ti found that the traditions of the past, embodied in the writings of scholars, had become so powerful that they were blocking the way to social changes he wished to make. So he ordered all books to be burned except for technical manuals and handbooks. Only 70 men in the whole country, those with the rank of Scholar of Great Learning, were allowed to keep books of philosophy and history, among them the writings of the Confucian school. Anyone else who had not burned his books within 30 days was branded and sent to work on the Great Wall.

The Chin dynasty was overthrown in 206 B.C., and a new

The mandarins who governed the Chinese empire wore special costumes indicating their position and rank. The bird embroidered on this mandarin's gown shows that he is a civil rather than a military official.

dynasty, the Han, was founded. During the reign of the Han emperors, the books destroyed by Shih Huang Ti were reconstructed. The teachings of Confucius, restored to their former importance, were declared state doctrine by Emperor Han Wu Ti in the second century B.C. Confucius had taught that government officials should be chosen for their abilities and not for their noble birth, and by 100 B.C., civil service exams were used to select the scholars and administrators who would manage public affairs. Even a peasant's son could rise through the ranks of the government bureaucracy. The civil service exam was much more than a test of reading, writing, and mathematical ability. Candidates had to have a thorough knowledge of philosophy and history and also an ability to write beautiful prose and poetry. At a time when most of Europe was still barbarian, learning was being encouraged throughout China. Intellectual achievements were rewarded, and the ideals of great thinkers were honored.

During the early years of her long history, China was completely cut off from the rest of the world, partly because of geography and partly because of Chinese attitudes toward outsiders. China thought of herself as the proud and noble center of the world, and she wanted nothing to do with the barbarians beyond her boundaries. But as civilizations developed in the rest of the world, contact could not always be avoided. During the Han dynasty, trade routes to the West were established, and caravans carried Chinese silk to the outposts of the Roman Empire. Beginning around the third century A.D., the religion of Buddhism began to filter into China from many different sources; in the sixth century, the emperor sent a messenger to India to get the true text of the Buddha's teachings. In the 13th century, Genghis Khan and his conquering hordes swept in from Mongolia and seized control of China, which remained part of the Mongol Empire for 200 years. In 1272, a family of Venetian merchants— the brothers Maffio and Niccolo Polo, and Niccolo's son, Marco— set out on an overland journey to China which lasted three years. During the 17 years that the Polos remained in China, Marco served as an agent of the Great Khan Kublai and traveled to many parts of the country. Marco Polo's book about his experiences in China, written after his return, provided the first detailed information Westerners had about the size and power of the strange country known to them as Cathay.

About 1650, China made contact with Russia across the 2,000 miles of steppe, desert, and forest that lay between the two countries. Chinese junks sailed along the coast of the South China Sea and began trading with countries such as Vietnam, Siam, Malaya, and Indonesia. Some went farther, sailing into the Indian Ocean to India, Arabia, and the coast of Africa.

2. *East Meets West*

In the 15th century, Europe's sailor-adventurers began to roam the world in search of riches and conquests, and merchants and sovereigns commissioned sea captains to find a sea route to the fabled riches of the Orient. Columbus was on such a quest when he stumbled on America by accident. He had set out to find a westerly route to the Orient and believed that his landfall in the Caribbean was an island off the coast of China.

Soon after Columbus's venture into the New World, European merchants put into Canton, the only Chinese port open to foreigners. The Portuguese reached Canton in 1516, the Dutch in 1624, and the British in 1637.

The Chinese, still with a deep sense of their own superiority, had no intention of allowing Western barbarians into the Celestial Empire. But they were tempted by the prospect of trading China's silks, porcelain, tea, and works of art for the furs, sandalwood, exotic food, and aromatic herbs which the Westerners could provide. So they arranged an ingenious and complicated system of trade. Macao (Mah-KAUW), a city on the seaward tip of a river delta leading 85 miles up to Canton, was leased to the Portuguese. All foreign ships had to stop here, put their women ashore, and receive from the Chinese government a "chop," or permit with an official seal. This allowed them to proceed upriver for search and inspection by Chinese officials.

The European ships next had to dock at Whampoa Island. There they paid their port charges and engaged an agent and interpreter through whom all business with Chinese merchants had to be conducted. They also made arrangements for a hong merchant—a representative of a Chinese merchants' association —to meet them in Canton. At Whampoa, cargo had to be transferred from the large ocean-going vessels to smaller river boats, which then made their way 12 miles up the river to Canton.

At Canton the boats docked at the European merchants' compound outside the walls of the city. Trading was limited to this half-mile-square area, in which were located 13 large "factories" —trading stations made up of warehouses, counting houses, offices, and apartments for the visiting foreigners. (The word *factory* in this usage is derived from *factor*, the name for an agent who transacts business for another.)

All business conducted in the European factories had to be negotiated through the appointed hong merchant, who represented a merchants' association called the co-hong. The co-hong was an important element in the Chinese trading system. It fixed the prices for all foreign goods brought into China and was responsible for the actions of the foreign traders while they were in Canton. Members of the association were supported by the full power of China's massive bureaucracy. They were backed by the provincial officials headed by the local viceroy, who was in

The European merchants' compound at Canton. The flags of many Western nations flew over the factories where the foreign traders conducted their business with the Chinese merchants.

turn supported by the authority of the Imperial Throne and the Celestial Emperor.

The control exerted by the hong merchants, as well as the endless complications of seals, permits, and restrictions, proved very useful to the Chinese. The system gave them the benefit of monopoly trade with the outside world without allowing foreigners to gain a foothold on the Chinese mainland. To further restrict the foreign influence, the Chinese kept the European traders virtual prisoners while they were in Canton. Only on rare occasions were the visitors allowed to leave the trading compound and then only when escorted by their Chinese hosts. On the 8th, 18th, and 28th days of the moon, parties of no more than 10 people at a time were allowed to visit the flower gardens of Fati, across the Canton River.

One or two Westerners risked instant death by sneaking into Canton in disguise. They brought back colorful tales of a vital city, both majestic and squalid. Exotic sights and sounds surrounded the foreigner in Canton: shrines to Buddha; enormous statues of gilded wood; the sound of gongs and the scent of burning incense; battles between street gangs; whole families living on sampans in the river; flower-decked boats for mandarins and their attendants; and wandering peddlers like the fish sellers, who carried their wares in tubs of water suspended from bamboo poles over their shoulders.

Americans were not among the foreign visitors to Canton until fairly late in the period of the China trade. During the colonial era, British commerce with China was monopolized by the powerful East India Company; American ships were not free to take part in the China trade until the War of Independence had been fought and won. By then, East Coast merchants were urgently in need of new markets. As quickly as they could, American shippers plunged into the China trade.

The *Empress of China* was the first ship to leave the United

States for Canton. She sailed in 1784 from New York, going east and south around the Cape of Good Hope at the tip of South America. Her 30-ton cargo consisted mostly of furs and ginseng (JIN-seng), a rare root used in Chinese medicine. She brought back a cargo of tea, porcelain, silk, cinnamon, and nankeen—a kind of cotton cloth used for men's trousers.

The following year, the first American millionaire, Elias Hasket Derby, started on the road to fortune by way of the China trade. He dispatched the merchantman *Grand Turk* from Salem, Massachusetts, with a cargo of flour, rice, butter, cheese, sugar, chocolate, prunes, beef, bacon, ham, fish, claret, brandy, rum, cognac, beer, earthenware, oil, candles, soap, aniseed, ginseng, tar, and bars of iron. Part of this cargo was sold on the island of Mauritius in the Indian Ocean and replaced with ebony, gold thread, cloth, betel nuts, and more ginseng. The remaining goods were traded in Canton for porcelain and tea. Derby made 100 percent profit on the round trip.

The merchantman *Grand Turk*, one of the first American ships to sail to Canton. Before the *Grand Turk* entered the China trade, she had pursued a successful career as a privateer, capturing 16 foreign merchant ships for the American government.

The American trade with China developed rapidly, still operating only through the tightly controlled port of Canton. American ships scoured the South Seas for delicacies to delight the luxurious tastes of the Chinese mandarins. They shipped birds' nests, sharks' fins, and *bêche-de-mer* (sea slugs) for soups, sandalwood for its scent, tortoiseshell and mother-of-pearl for ornaments. Furs were also a highly profitable item of trade. Sable, fox, ermine, beaver, and sea otter pelts could be bought from the Indians in Vancouver and Alaska for a few cents' worth of iron and sold in China for $100 or more.

By 1789, as many as 15 United States flagships could be seen in Canton harbor at one time. They came from such East Coast ports as Boston, Salem, Providence, New York, Philadelphia, and Baltimore, most of them stopping to trade at intermediate ports on the way. Some made the voyage around Cape Horn and traveled all the way up the western seaboard of the Americas to collect furs from Vancouver and Alaska. Then they sailed across the Pacific to Canton. Others went eastward, across the Atlantic and Indian oceans.

At home in the United States, *chinoiserie* (sheen-wahz-uh-REE) —art and decoration in the Chinese style—was becoming all the rage. Fashionable New Englanders paid good prices for teakwood chests, lacquered tables, jade and ivory ornaments, porcelain, silks, bronze, copper, feather brushes, fans mounted with mother-of-pearl, and miniature pagodas decorated with gold leaf.

3. *The Opium War*

During this period, many other nations were also trading with China through Canton, with the British predominant among them. It was the British traders who first introduced opium into China, originally for use in medicine. When the Chinese discovered its uses as an escapist drug, the opium trade boomed, with Americans supplying a small 5 percent of the total volume.

By 1800, so many of China's 250 million people had become addicted to opium that the emperor passed an imperial edict forbidding the importation of this "vile dust." The British East India Company formally agreed not to bring any more opium into China, but nevertheless it took part in the huge illegal trade in opium which quickly developed.

In addition to the illegal opium trade, there were other sources of conflict between China and the Western nations during this period. Foreign sailors were now allowed to go ashore in Canton. They were becoming involved in brawls, assaults, and murders in the grogshops of Hog Lane, the section of Canton set aside for their entertainment. Decisions about who should try and punish these men caused serious international friction.

Late in 1838, the Chinese government decided to wipe out the opium trade. High Commissioner Lin Tse-hue, the official in charge of suppressing the trade, came to Canton and ordered all foreign and Chinese traders to cease dealing in opium on pain of death. The death sentence was also to be enforced against anyone who grew, sold, or smoked opium. When the British, Americans, and other Westerners announced their intention of defying this ruling, Chinese troops surrounded the trading compound. They kept its occupants under siege for six weeks, while both sides attempted to settle the dispute by negotiation. Finally the Westerners surrendered the opium in their possession, and the siege was lifted.

In 1839, a drunken brawl and a murder involving British sailors set off the first open conflict between the British and the Chinese in the so-called Opium War. Chinese officials, accompanied by a fleet of war junks, approached the British fleet and demanded that the murderers be turned over to them for punishment. The British replied by firing on the Chinese ships and sinking them. Protesting the incident, High Commissioner Lin sent an angry message to Queen Victoria: "You savages of the further seas have waxed so bold, it seems, as to defy and insult our mighty empire. . . . If you continue in your path of obstinate delusion, your three islands will be laid waste and your people pounded into mincemeat." In reply, Queen Victoria sent 16 warships, 27 troopships, and 4,000 soldiers to China.

In June 1840, the British forces blockaded Canton and Ningpo, a port in China's busy central area. The following year they captured Canton and the river forts protecting it and advanced inland, making steady progress against the fierce but ill-equipped Chinese army. Eventually the emperor in Peking surrendered. In accordance with the terms of the Nanking Treaty of 1842, which ended the war, China had to cede Hong Kong to the British, open up the ports of Amoy, Shanghai, Ningpo, and Foochow to international trade, abolish the hong system of trade monopoly, and pay a war indemnity of $21 million. Worse yet, the opium trade was resumed.

Following the Opium War, China suffered one indignity after another at the hands of the foreigners she had tried so long to keep out of the country. Englishmen, Frenchmen, Americans, Germans, and Russians demanded and took privileges and concessions until eventually they had taken over the right to try and punish Chinese nationals in their own land. American merchants, diplomats, missionaries, educators, and welfare workers poured into China. Some came for profit, others for unselfish reasons. But to the Chinese they were all suspect. The foreigners lived in segregated communities which were protected by treaties imposed from abroad and supported in times of stress by gunboats. Foreign mission boards obtained possession of land and property for missionary compounds, hospitals, churches, schools, and homes. Soon there were prosperous Little Americas scattered throughout China. Many of them were concentrated in the areas where the Western nations had established the extraterritorial privileges that were so resented by the Chinese.

4. Chinese Emigration in the 19th Century

During the 1840s and 1850s, Americans were not only going to China but some Chinese were also coming to the United States. At the same time that China was being forced to recognize the existence of the outside world, California was beginning to attract settlers. Although emigration from China was still officially illegal, two groups of Chinese people, from opposite ends of the social hierarchy, had begun to make their way to the United States: students and intellectuals came to study in American schools, and unskilled laborers came in search of work in the gold mines and on the railroads.

In 1868, the doors were officially opened for Americans to travel to China and for Chinese to travel to the United States. In that year, Anson Burlingame, an American diplomat who had become a trusted adviser to the Chinese government, negotiated a treaty between the two countries. By the terms of the Burlingame Treaty, both China and the United States recognized "the inherent and inalienable right of man to change his home and allegiance and also the mutual advantage of free migration and emigration of their citizens and subjects respectively, from one country to the other, for the purpose of curiosity, of trade or as permanent residents."

The freedom of migration guaranteed by the Burlingame Treaty proved very useful to the Chinese people during the turbulent years following the Opium War. By the middle of the 19th century, China was in a sad state. The government of the Manchu dynasty, which had ruled the country since 1644, had become hopelessly ineffective. It was corrupt and brutal, with a bureaucracy so complicated that it prevented any useful action. Many of the mandarins, the ruling government officials, were dishonest; they extorted high taxes from the mass of people, who lived in misery and want. The Manchu rulers lived in their old

The Summer Palace of the Manchu emperors, outside Peking. By the middle of the 19th century, the Manchu dynasty had become weak and corrupt. Its rulers lived in isolated splendor while the Chinese people struggled against poverty and high taxes.

secluded way and quite failed to come to grips with the Westerners who had pushed their way into China.

Life became even more insecure in China when civil war broke out. In 1850 a secret society called the Taipings gathered support from Christian converts and the peasant masses and attacked the Manchus in Peking. The imperial army was too weak to put down the insurrection, and for the next nine years battles raged between the Taipings and the Manchu government. It is estimated that some 20 million people were killed during the conflict. By 1860 the Taipings controlled more than half of China, with the approval of the Americans and the British, who believed them to be a Christian organization. However, when the Taipings turned to more exotic forms of religion and the upheaval seemed likely to threaten trade with China, the Western nations helped to put down the Taiping insurrection.

Civil wars like the Taiping revolt were not new to the Chinese. Internal conflicts had been part of their history for centuries, as different groups of people speaking different dialects moved from one area of China to another. Nevertheless, the Taiping war made the poor peasants even poorer, so that when they heard of opportunities for work and good pay overseas they were more inclined to listen than they might otherwise have been.

China had many poor to meet the demand for labor that was growing around the world. Chinese laborers went to nearby Asian countries like Siam, Burma, Vietnam, Malaya, and the Philippines. Others crossed the Pacific to Hawaii and to California. A few were kidnapped and forced to work in foreign lands, but most left China by choice. Strong family loyalty was (and still is) a Chinese tradition, and the Chinese emigrants disliked leaving their homes. But many poor men felt it was their duty to leave in order to earn money to support their families in China. However, almost all went with the understanding that they would return home again in a few years' time.

Of those who came to the United States during these years, more than half were from the mountain city of Toishan in the district of Kwangtung in southern China. The people of Toishan were of pioneering stock, having made their way south from a northern area on the Yellow River. Their land was so poor that they could feed their own community for only four months in the year. As a result, they had turned to trade, acting as middlemen and merchants and traveling to other cities and to the ports of the Canton River delta. In this way they met the white traders, saw their ships, and heard of opportunities to make money overseas. As immigrants in the United States began to send money back to Toishan, together with reports of the steady work available, more men left to join them.

5. The Birth of Modern China

At the beginning of the 20th century, China was still in a miserable state. Civil war divided the country, the government was weak, and foreigners were playing an increasingly important role in Chinese commerce, education, and religion. Most Chinese industry was controlled by foreigners who lived in Shanghai; in that city there were European racecourses, clubs, and resorts where Chinese people were allowed only as servants. Not surprisingly, the Chinese resented being treated like aliens in their own country. In 1900 the Boxers, a secret brotherhood pledged to kill the white man, started a purge of Westerners in China. Many foreigners took refuge within the walls of Peking; they were besieged there for two months until an international army was able to reach the city and rescue them.

In 1908 the Manchu dowager empress Tzu-Hsi, who had held power for 50 years, died and was succeeded by a three-year-old child. On the 10th of October, 1911 — a date which the Chinese today commemorate as a national holiday called the Double Tenth — a riot started in the Yangtze Valley which government troops were unable to suppress. Administrators and mandarins

American marines march through a courtyard in Peking's Forbidden City during the Boxer Rebellion, 1900. The American forces were part of an international army sent to rescue Westerners trapped in Peking.

of the Manchu dynasty were murdered throughout China, and centuries of rule based on the Confucian principles came to an end.

For the next 38 years China was to have no stable government. After the overthrow of the Manchu dynasty, Sun Yat-sen, one of the rebel leaders, was named president of the new Chinese republic. But the republican forces controlled only the southern part of China. Less than a year after he assumed the presidency, Sun Yat-sen was persuaded to abdicate in favor of a Manchu military leader who promised to unify the divided country. In 1916, the Manchu leader died, leaving China without a ruler. A dozen warlords then seized power in different areas and fought cruel and senseless battles for control of the nation. Life was cheap and death became a spectacle, with mass beheadings drawing large crowds.

Gradually, Sun Yat-sen, supported by rioting students, built up the Nationalist Party, the Kuomintang, which by 1924 was gaining strength in Canton. The Nationalists believed that the Chinese people had to fight in order to throw out the warlords and the foreign imperialists. Russia, now communist, was the only nation to offer help. She sent an adviser, Michael Borodin, who persuaded Sun Yat-sen to let the 430 members of the Chinese Communist Party join the Nationalist cause.

In preparation for their struggle against the enemies of China, the Nationalists trained military officers to fight for their country instead of personal gain. Chiang Kai-shek was one of these officers. His American-educated wife, Mei-ling Soong, was a woman of great charm and beauty whose sister was married to Sun Yat-sen. When Sun Yat-sen died in 1925, Chiang Kai-shek seized the leadership of the Nationalist Party. Among the peasants and workers who rallied to his fight against the warlords was the communist intellectual Mao Tse-tung, then aged 33.

In four years the membership of the Chinese Communist

Japanese troops standing on a rooftop give the victory signal after the fall of Shanghai in 1937.

Party grew to 60,000, and a split developed between the Communists and the Nationalists. In 1927 Chiang's troops tried to suppress the Communists by a purge in Shanghai, and once again China was at war with herself, torn between the two parties. Guerrilla warfare continued until the Communists and Nationalists were temporarily united by a common enemy, Japan. Having already won control of mineral-rich Manchuria in 1932, Japan attacked the rest of China in 1936.

Shanghai was the first city to fall to the Japanese. Nanking was sacked, and the prosperous cities of the Yangtze Valley were ravaged. In the world's first mass bombing raids aimed at a civilian population, Japan bombed the Nationalists and the Communists in their separate mountain strongholds. Both parties fought against the Japanese without much success. Then, in the few hours it took the Japanese to bomb Pearl Harbor, the American naval base in Hawaii, China's fortunes changed. From that time on, the full power of the United States and her European allies supported the Chinese in their battle with Japan.

American planes protected the Chinese armies from Japanese bombers and flew in supplies over the Himalayas. American officers helped to train and strengthen Chiang Kai-shek's army, but their help was refused by the Communists. Then in 1945 the atom bombs dropped on Hiroshima and Nagasaki forced the

Japanese to surrender, and World War II was over.

After the war American diplomats worked hard to reconcile the Chinese Nationalist and Communist parties or even to get them to agree to a peaceful partition of China. But there was no way in which the two sides could live together. In 1948 the Communists launched a new offensive, and by the next year the Nationalists were defeated. Westerners fled from Shanghai. Chiang Kai-shek and his Nationalist followers retreated to the island of Taiwan (Formosa), where they received American support and tried to rebuild their army.

After 1949, China was once again cut off from the rest of the world. Her people were not free to leave the country when they wished. Foreign visitors were strictly controlled. The nation worked alone, trying to bring health, education, and prosperity to her 580 million people, most of whom had never known anything better than crushing poverty.

In 1951, when China entered the Korean War, the United States Foreign Assets Control Board ruled that no more money could be sent from the United States to mainland China. Chinese immigrants had sent money to their families back home ever since their earliest days in America, but now these contributions ceased completely. Chinese people in the United States had to face up to the fact that for them China was no longer home.

Then in the early 1970s, China's relationship with the rest of the world began to change. In November 1971, the United Nations General Assembly voted to admit mainland China and to expel the Nationalist government of Taiwan, which had been the only representative of the Chinese people in the United Nations for more than 20 years. As in the past, the United States opposed Communist China's admission. However, the startling announcement made a few months earlier of President Richard Nixon's plans to visit China suggested to many that the United States was ready for a new era of Chinese-American relations.

President and Mrs. Richard M. Nixon visit the Great Wall of China, February 1972. They are accompanied by a group of reporters and interpreters.

In February 1972, the historic journey took place. President Nixon spent a week in China, conferring privately with the country's leaders and visiting some of the landmarks of its ancient civilization. Upon his return to the United States, the president declared that the goal of his visit—the reestablishment of communications with China—had been accomplished. The link was a fragile one, but it offered hope for the future. Chinese Americans might one day be able to renew their own contacts with the homeland of their ancestors.

PART II

Land of the Golden Mountains

1. *Early Settlers in California*

When American ships began trading across the Pacific into the Chinese ports opened after the Opium War, California was still a province of Mexico. One of the visitors to the California coast during this period was Richard Henry Dana, an 18-year-old Bostonian who dropped out of Harvard in 1834 and went to sea in the brig *Pilgrim*. His book *Two Years before the Mast* gives a contemporary account of some of California's coastal settlements during the years of Mexican rule. Most of the people Dana saw were descendants of Spaniards and Indians. They lived in small adobe villages strategically placed near ports which were stopping places for coastal ships trading in hides, furs, tallow (animal fat), and wine.

San Diego was one of the liveliest settlements along the California coast. In this thriving community, Dana met people from all over the world—Mexican settlers, Hawaiian sailors from the Sandwich Islands, European traders from Germany, France, Scotland, Italy, and Spain. Other settlements existed at Los Angeles, Santa Barbara, San Gabriel, Monterey, and Yerba Buena, the early name for San Francisco. When Dana first came to the California coast, the tiny community at Yerba Buena consisted only of an adobe settlement house, a few small dwellings, and a chapel. But the bay on which the settlement was located proved to be a convenient meeting place for Russian, English, and American whalers, and an ideal port for brigs like the *Pilgrim*, trading in furs and tallow. When Dana returned to San Francisco 24 years later, it had become a city with a population of 100,000.

The Mexican era in California ended in the late 1840s, with the outbreak of war between Mexico and the United States. Mexico was defeated, and in 1848 she signed a peace treaty ceding New Mexico, California, and Arizona to the United States. That same year, gold was discovered in California on the land of a settler named John Sutter. A new period of western history was about to begin.

John Sutter was one of California's early settlers. He owned a large area of land in the Sacramento Valley which he had named New Helvetia, in honor of the homeland of his Swiss parents. (Helvetia was the Roman name for Switzerland.) On his vast holdings, Sutter established orchards, wheatfields, grazing fields for stock, and a sawmill, and he took a loving pride in their development. Then in January 1848, a carpenter named James Marshall found hunks of gold in the pond of Sutter's sawmill. Sutter tried to keep the discovery of gold secret, for he realized that once it was made public, his homestead would be threatened with ruin. But a rich gold strike generates too much fever to be concealed for long, and the news spread rapidly. Soon Sutter's land had been trampled over, his orchards stripped, and his cattle slaughtered by men who came to look for gold and helped themselves to anything they found along the way.

In 1848, the year that gold was discovered at Sutter's mill, the population of California was about 15,000. Two years later, it had grown to 150,000. During these years, hundreds of trappers, farmers, merchants, homesteaders, and miners had come hurrying west along the Mormon, Oregon, and California trails. They came first by wagon and later by commercial stagecoach. An express coach, traveling day and night, could make the journey from St. Louis to San Francisco in one month. Some made the journey to California by sea, sailing from the East Coast of the

During the California gold rush, hundreds of ships were left abandoned in San Francisco Bay while their crews joined in the search for gold.

United States around Cape Horn. This route took about four months, sometimes even six or eight months if the winds were unfavorable. Others sailed south to Panama and marched across the isthmus, despite the risk of yellow fever there. They embarked again on the Pacific coast to complete their journey to California.

As word spread of the gold in the California hills, fortune hunters from all over the world made their way to San Francisco as fast as they could. Within six years of the discovery at Sutter's mill, 400 ships could be seen at anchor in San Francisco Bay, more than half of them abandoned as their captains and crews joined the rush for gold.

2. *California Beckons to the Chinese*

Chinese merchants trading out of San Francisco quickly carried home news of the gold strike in California. In Chinese villages stories were told of the Gum San—land of the Golden Mountains—where gold was lying on the ground just waiting to be picked up. In the heavily populated province of Kwangtung, around the Canton River estuary, interest in the California gold strike was especially high. Many Kwangtung villagers defied their government's rule against leaving the country and set sail for San Francisco.

Soon transport from China to California became highly organized—and profitable. Most people traveled from Hong Kong, where Chinese brokers would arrange their passage on credit. The voyage itself cost about $50, but the broker's expenses, interest charges, and often sheer extortion inflated the price, sometimes to as much as $200. Yet many Chinese cheerfully agreed to pay this amount, confident that they would soon be rich enough to repay the loan without hardship. In fact, it often took five or six years to pay off the cost of the passage.

Some Chinese immigrants made the voyage comfortably in fast ships; others had a miserable passage in leaky old hulks which could take as long as four months to get to California. On arrival in San Francisco, new immigrants were met by representatives of the Chinese Six Companies, associations representing the six districts in Kwangtung from which most of the Chinese immigrants came. New arrivals were sorted into groups speaking the same dialect and then offered accommodation in dormitories. In this way, the immigrants usually found themselves living with people who came from the same area back home and who could help to make their new life less confusing.

Some of the Chinese immigrants came specifically to look for gold. Others came to work as farm laborers or to find jobs in the many service industries that catered to the rapidly growing population on the West Coast. At this time, unskilled laborers in California could make two to five dollars a day, which seemed more than adequate to Chinese workers who had been lucky to get 10 cents a day back home.

A circular published in 1862 by one of Hong Kong's many

passage brokers illustrates the kind of incentives used to encourage Chinese immigration to the United States.

> To the countrymen of Au Chan! There are laborers wanted in the land of Oregon, in the United States, in America. There is much inducement to go to this new country, as they have many great works there which are not in our own country. They will supply good houses and plenty of food. They will pay you $28 a month after your arrival, and treat you considerately when you arrive. There is no fear of slavery. All is nice. The ship is now going and will take all who can pay their passage. The money required is $54. Persons having property can have it sold for them by correspondents, or borrow money of me upon security. I cannot take security on your children or your wife. Come to me in Hong Kong and I will care for you until you start. The ship is substantial and convenient.
>
> *Au Chan*

From the beginning of Chinese immigration in the 1840s to the passage of the Chinese Exclusion Act in 1882, approximately 300,000 Chinese immigrants entered the United States. More than half of this number returned to China within a few years. In the year 1860, about 35,000 Chinese came to the United States; 63,000 came in 1870, and 105,000 in 1880. In 1882, the year that the Exclusion Act was passed, 132,000 Chinese immigrants entered the United States.

3. *In the Goldfields*

In the 1840s and 1850s, the greatest incentive for Chinese immigration to the United States was the lure of the California goldfields. But the immigrants' dream of fortune and success in the land of the Golden Mountains did not always come true. Life in the goldfields was rough, tough, and fiercely competitive. First-comers staked their claims, went over the ground in search of large pieces of gold, and then moved on to fresh claims, often fighting for the best sites. In the years 1849 and 1850, the yield of gold averaged about $600 for each miner. However, this figure is only an average: some became rich beyond their wildest dreams, while many more were disappointed. Some miners lost all they had made in the games of chance, drunken brawls, and murders which were commonplace in San Francisco. This city, the metropolis of the gold rush, grew at a speed no law enforcement could keep pace with.

As the gold rush continued, prices for goods and services in California rose astronomically. For instance, freight rates for the sea voyage between New York and San Francisco went from $13 a ton in 1849 to $60 a ton in 1850. One round trip paid a ship owner enough to recover the cost of his ship.

Of the foreigners who came to California in search of gold, only the Irish outnumbered the Chinese, with Germans as the next largest group. Men also flooded in from Spain, Mexico, Russia, and many other countries. When Chinese immigrants arrived in California on their way to the goldfields, they went first to the Six Companies in San Francisco for advice and help. The immigrants quickly learned that they had a choice of action. They could stake claims in the goldfields and work on their own, or they could work as assistants to established miners and be content to keep one-half of all the gold they found. If they preferred, the Chinese immigrants could also take jobs in one of the many service industries either in the mining camps or in San Francisco, where there was good money to be made by skilled carpenters and by workers in laundries, restaurants, and hotels.

Many Chinese miners made rich strikes and steady incomes.

Chinese workers mining gold in California. The man in the foreground is using a device called a "cradle" to separate pieces of gold from worthless stone and gravel.

Because of their cultural background and training, they had that quiet diligence which gave them the patience to work slowly over land which had already been stripped of its biggest nuggets. Thus they were able to find quantities of small particles and of gold dust which were enough to make them rich.

The Chinese were subjected to many jokes and cruelties in the goldfields, often just because they looked so different from the other miners. They were set apart by their distinctive physical appearance and their traditional Chinese clothes—blue nankeen blouses, baggy trousers, cloth slippers, and wide straw hats. Chinese men also wore waist-long pigtails known as queues (KEWS). This hairstyle was a symbol of subjection which had been forced on the Chinese people when the Manchus seized power in the 17th century. The Chinese in the United States kept their queues as insurance that they could go back to China whenever they wished. However, when the Manchu government was overthrown in 1911, Chinese men everywhere immediately cut off their queues as a sign of liberty and independence.

In the early years of the gold rush, many Chinese people returned home after a while, taking the money they had made back to their families. Some found it hard to settle down again and returned to California for another spell in the goldfields. But it became increasingly difficult to make a good income there. Claims were harder to stake. Moreover, because so much of the ground had been worked over, all that remained was either very fine gold dust or deposits lying well below the surface. Gradually miners returned home or drifted into other industries. By about 1873, the goldfields of California were more or less worked out.

4. *Building the Railroad*

Even before the gold in California ran out, a new demand for Chinese workers had already arisen. The Six Companies in San Francisco had been asked to find labor to help build a new railroad which would cross the western half of the continent. In the early 1860s, a transcontinental railroad seemed to provide an answer to many of the nation's needs. A much faster means of transportation was needed to link the old wealth of the East Coast with the new wealth of the West. Trade with China could be speeded up if goods could make an overland journey across the United States. Then, too, the outbreak of the Civil War in 1860 made Congress eager to bind the West to the Union with a railroad link. In 1862, President Abraham Lincoln approved the Pacific Railway Bill, which authorized the Union Pacific Company to start building a rail line westward from Omaha, Nebraska, and the Central Pacific Company to start building eastward from Sacramento, California.

The building of the transcontinental railroad took place long before the days of heavy machinery; all the work had to be done by hand, with picks, shovels, crowbars, axes, sledgehammers, blasting powder, wheelbarrows, and one-horse dump carts. An enormous labor force was needed, and it had to be recruited in competition with the lure of the easy money to be made in the California goldfields and in other areas throughout the West where mineral strikes were being made.

Even when construction crews could be hired, the problems of building the railroad were just beginning. The Central Pacific Company had by far the more difficult task. A few miles out of Sacramento, the railroad had to climb into the high ridges of the Sierra Nevada, saw-toothed mountains of granite which rise to 9,000 and 10,000 feet. The work was hard and discouraging. As fast as Charles Crocker, the director of construction, hired men and sent them up into the hills, they quit for easier ways of making a living. In the early days, only 1 in 10 stayed on the job for more than a week. Somewhere Crocker had to find the 5,000 men he needed. Thus it was that in 1865 he asked for the help of the Chinese Six Companies.

Crocker's construction superintendent did not believe that the slightly built Chinese would be strong enough for such heavy work, but he agreed to hire a trial group. Oscar Lewis describes the result of the experiment in his book on the building of the railroad, *The Big Four:*

> Fifty Chinese were hired. They were hauled to the end of the track. They disembarked, glanced without curiosity at the surrounding forest, then tranquilly established camp, cooked a meal of rice and dried cuttlefish and went to sleep. By sunrise, they were at work with picks, shovels and wheel-barrows. At the end of their first twelve hours of plodding industry, Crocker and his engineers viewed the result with gratified astonishment.

The Central Pacific began to hire Chinese people living on the West Coast, sending them to the railhead in groups of 50. The Chinese soon earned a reputation as disciplined, tireless, and energetic workers. They cut trees, rooted out stumps, broke and carted rock, graded the roadbed, put down ties, and spiked home the rails, working with burly Irishmen who handled the lengths of iron. They produced the longest and smoothest stretches of grading on those rugged mountains.

As the construction crews moved higher into the Sierra Nevada, the mountains became steeper and sheerer, and it became increasingly difficult to cut a path through them. The Chinese workers, however, found a way to solve this problem. From reeds gathered in San Francisco Bay they wove round baskets with waist-high sides. One or two Chinese workmen were lowered in these baskets by rope and pulley down the side of a sheer cliff. They chipped holes in the rock, packed in blasting powder, and were hauled rapidly to safety before the powder blasted out another foothold for workers to enlarge into the bed of the railroad.

At times the Central Pacific construction crews were tunneling through solid granite, working day and night in eight-hour shifts. When the winter snow came, much of the work had to stop, but a number of the Chinese went on. They worked and lived completely under the snow, keeping air shafts and access tunnels open. Somewhere between 500 and 1,000 were killed by avalanches, falls, and accidents of various kinds.

Six months after the first Chinese started work on the railroad, 2,000 Chinese laborers had been hired. Soon the Central Pacific was contracting with shipping companies to bring workers directly from China. By 1866, there were 10,000 Chinese working on the railroad. A year later the total Central Pacific labor force consisted of 14,000 men; of these, 12,000 were Chinese, most of them by now veteran railroad builders. Charles Crocker thought so highly of his Chinese workers that they were known universally as "Crocker's Pets."

The Chinese laborers organized themselves into crews of 12 to 20 men, often keeping a few spare workers so that even if someone got sick, they could turn out with a full crew. Each crew lived together in tents or huts; each had its own cook and its own Chinese head-man, who kept discipline. The Chinese workers imported their own groceries—dried oysters, abalone, bamboo shoots, bean sprouts, crackers, noodles, Chinese bacon and pork, poultry, and tea. They ate sumptuously in comparison with the white workers, who usually had boiled beef, bread, potatoes, and coffee. The Chinese bathed each night after work and changed into clean clothes before supper, customs which amazed their white fellow workers.

While the Chinese workers of the Central Pacific struggled to push the railroad through the Sierra Nevada, the Union Pacific, working over the plains from Omaha, was having a much easier time of it. Most of the workers on the Union Pacific were Irish, and they held the track-laying record—eight miles of track in a single day. Crocker was confident, however, that once the Central Pacific was over the mountains, his Chinese workers could beat the Union Pacific record. Just before the last few miles of track were to be laid, Crocker put together a hand-picked team which completed 10 miles of track in one day and so captured the record.

In his speech at the celebration held when the two sections of railroad met in 1869, Crocker praised his Chinese workers: ". . . The early completion of this railroad we have built has been in a great measure due to that poor, destitute class of laborers called the Chinese—to the fidelity and industry they have shown. . . ."

When the railroad was finished, 25,000 men lost their jobs and began competing with each other for whatever other work was available. Many of the Chinese workers went back to China or to Hawaii, where there were jobs to be found on the sugar plantations. However, at the same time even more were arriving in the United States. Immigration records show that 60,000 Chinese returned home between 1868 and 1877, but 130,000

The first transcontinental train leaves Sacramento, California, in 1869. Its departure is hailed by some of the Chinese workers who helped to lay the miles of track over which it would travel. (*Thomas Gilcrease Institute*)

more came to America during these years. Some took jobs picking fruit and tomatoes, and again their virtues as workers were appreciated. In 1870, one-tenth of all farm labor on the West Coast was Chinese. Ten years later one-third was Chinese, and by 1884 fully one-half of the farm labor force in California was Chinese. But often this was seasonal work which left thousands unemployed for months at a time.

Many Chinese worked on reclamation of land around San Francisco Bay. Others went into domestic service or took jobs in cigar and woolen factories and in various service industries in the cities. But on the West Coast in the 1870s there were too many people chasing too few jobs. The Chinese were hit harder than most by the depressed economic situation.

5. *"Not a Chinaman's Chance"*

Even during the boom years, Chinese people in the United States were often treated badly by others simply because they were different. The objects of popular prejudice, they were despised because of their appearance, their culture, their religion. To many Americans the Chinese were heathens who wore inscrutable expressions, jabbered an incomprehensible language, and ate weird food. Perhaps most unforgivable of all, they chose to keep themselves apart from other people and did not even try to integrate into the existing American society.

There were reasons for the self-imposed isolation of the Chinese immigrants. They had come from an ancient, highly organized culture at the heart of which was a strong family structure supported by duty and obedience. Most of the Chinese laborers who came to the United States were simple, uneducated men traveling without their families; they found the American way of life and thinking so different from their own that they were completely baffled. So they tried to preserve their old life style by huddling together in the Chinatowns that grew up in many American cities. After all, they expected to be in the United

The distinctive appearance and dress of the Chinese immigrants often made them the objects of popular prejudice. The Chinese miners in this old photograph are set apart from their white fellow-workers by their queues, worn wound around the backs of their heads, and by their loose-fitting clothes and large straw hats.

States for a few years only and then to return to their families in China. This was a completely different attitude from that of other immigrants, most of whom arrived committed to a new life in the United States.

The isolation of the Chinese immigrants and the uniqueness of their life style seemed to arouse fear and hatred in many situations. In the goldfields Chinese miners were robbed, beaten, and cheated. Miners of many other nationalities received similar treatment, but the Chinese were often picked on as a group. Their experiences in the goldfields gave rise to the expression "not a Chinaman's chance." In the 1850s and '60s, someone who didn't even have "a Chinaman's chance" for success in an undertaking was certainly doomed to failure.

During this period the Chinese immigrants were not allowed to become United States citizens, so they had no vote. In some areas they were even denied the protection of the courts. In 1854 an ugly mood of white supremacy in California pushed through a state law prohibiting "people of color"—Asians, Negroes, and Indians—from testifying against a white person in court.

When economic conditions on the West Coast began to decline, the position of the Chinese became even more difficult. In the 1870s, men continued to pour into the area, even though the goldfields were worked out and the railroad was completed. They had either not heard or not believed that the boom was over and that thousands already there were out of work. Wages for what jobs there were became depressed. Eventually the frustration and bitterness of men who had arrived with such high hopes turned to violence.

All too often the Chinese were made the scapegoats for other men's frustration. Competition for jobs was intense, and the Chinese were accused of shutting out white labor by accepting low pay, and of lowering standards of living. Some Chinese laborers, desperate for work and excluded from the trade unions, had allowed themselves to be used as strikebreakers on the East Coast. Industrialists in Massachusetts, New Jersey, and Pennsylvania had brought them from the West Coast to take over the jobs of workers who were out on strike. The anger that this caused in the labor movement increased the vicious attacks already being directed at Chinese immigrants throughout the United States.

They were robbed, mobbed, burned out of their homes, beaten, and lynched so often that they seldom dared to go outside their own domain in Chinatown. A Chinese man walking alone could expect to be attacked by thugs, or even by schoolboys. Bret Harte, a California writer, wrote an obituary for the victim of one such attack: "Dead, my reverend friends, dead, stoned to death in the streets of San Francisco in the year of grace 1869 by a mob of half-grown boys and Christian schoolchildren."

Ringleader of the terrorism in San Francisco was Denis Kearney, head of the Workingman's Party. Kearney specialized in fiery speeches denouncing the Chinese as enemies of American workers. Roused by the slogan "The Chinese must go," his mobs ransacked Chinatown, where 116,000 Chinese people lived in fear.

The Chinese were also victims of violence in other California cities. In 1871 a group was lynched by a mob in Los Angeles. Eight white rioters were convicted of the crime and received sentences varying from two to six years. Within a year all had been released from jail.

Outside of California, the story was the same. In the Union Pacific coal mines in Rock Springs, Wyoming, 331 Chinese worked alongside 150 whites. In 1885, an argument over which group should dig which vein of coal developed into a brawl and then into a massacre. The white miners, many armed with Winchester carbines, killed 28 Chinese miners, wounded 15,

Chinese immigrants being attacked in Denver, Colorado, 1880. Violent anti-Chinese riots took place in many western towns during the 1870s and 1880s.

and chased the remainder out of town. No white casualties were reported. Sixteen whites were arrested, but all were released when the grand jury found that "no one was able to testify to a single criminal act by any white person that day."

The following year, 100 Chinese workers in the mines on Douglas Island, Alaska, were attacked by a mob, driven to the sea, and set adrift in a small schooner. There were anti-Chinese riots in Seattle, in Tacoma, and in other American cities, riots which often resulted in the burning of the Chinese quarter.

Although it must have often seemed so to them, Chinese people in the United States were not entirely without friends during these years of persecution. In 1869 a group of San Francisco citizens formed a Chinese Protective Society. They hired special police guards and met ships on which Chinese people were expected to arrive. But they received very little public support or money, and the society survived for only one year.

In the Seattle riot the captain of the Home Guard, George Kinnear, defied the mob and with his men escorted the Chinese to safety. In Los Angeles, Erskine Ross, who later became a federal judge, halted a rampaging mob in the Chinese quarter, which had been set on fire.

Mark Twain, who spent several years in California in the 1860s, took the part of the persecuted Chinese in some of his writings published during this period. In *Roughing It*, a travel book which describes his western adventures, Twain praised the character of the Chinese immigrants: "They are quiet, peaceable, tractable, free from drunkenness, and they are as industrious as the day is long. A disorderly Chinaman is rare and a lazy one does not exist. . . ." He went on to make an ironic and bitter comment on the treatment given the Chinese by American society:

> He is a great convenience to everybody — even to the worst class of white men, for he bears most of their sins, suffering fines for their petty thefts, imprisonment for their robberies, and death for their murders. Any white man can swear a Chinaman's life away in the courts, but no Chinaman can testify against a white man. Ours is the 'land of the free' — nobody denies that — nobody challenges it. (Maybe it is because we won't let other people testify.) As I write, news comes that in broad daylight in San Francisco, some boys have stoned an inoffensive Chinaman to death and that although a large crowd witnessed the shameful deed, no one interfered. . . .

Chinese people on the West Coast tried to fight for protection in the courts but found it useless. Many returned to China; others moved to New England, the Midwest, and the South. They migrated to large cities where they lived in tightly segregated Chinatowns, withdrawing socially, politically, and economically from the rest of society. Because of this, the Chinese, perhaps more than any other immigrant group in the United States, preserved and perpetuated their own culture and institutions.

PART III

Restriction of Chinese Immigration

1. *Discrimination Gets the Support of the Law*

Emma Lazarus was already a bit out of date in 1886 when she wrote her inscription for the Statue of Liberty: "Bring me your tired, your poor, your huddled masses yearning to breathe free." Four years earlier, Congress had closed the door to poor Chinese immigrants by the passage of the Chinese Exclusion Act. Students, merchants, teachers, officials, and travelers from China were still acceptable, but laborers were not. This was the first time that the United States government denied entry to people of any specific national origin.

The Chinese Exclusion Act and other laws which made life difficult for the Chinese in America grew out of the bitterness caused by the depression of the 1870s. Even while there was work for everyone, the California state legislature, in 1852, had levied a Foreign Miners' Tax of $20 a month. It applied to all foreigners, but in the rambling life of the goldfields many of them were hard to identify. The Chinese, however, looked so obviously foreign that they could rarely evade the tax. Also passed during this period was the state law which prevented Asians and other "people of color" from testifying against a white man in court.

By the time that persecution of Chinese people had become an obsession on the West Coast, legislators in the city of San Francisco, the state of California, and the United States Congress were giving in to the pressures of their electors and passing laws

This drawing shows three Chinese men being forced to do public penance for having cut off their queues. A similar fate awaited Chinese immigrants in the United States who returned to China without their queues.

that were openly prejudicial. Some of the laws were later struck down as biased and unconstitutional, but they caused much misery while they were in effect.

The Cubic Air Ordinance passed in 1871 attempted to legislate against overcrowding in San Francisco's Chinatown by specifying that each adult had to have a minimum of 500 cubic feet of living space. Hundreds of Chinese people were jailed for breaking the ordinance. Soon, however, the jails themselves became so overcrowded that they were found in violation of the same law, and it had to be abandoned.

That same year, a Queue Ordinance was introduced in San Francisco. This law required all prisoners in the city jails to have their hair cut so that it was no more than one inch long. Such a regulation was a cruel interference with the personal rights of a Chinese man, who needed his queue to be sure he could return to China without fear of punishment by the Manchus. The Queue Ordinance was finally repealed in 1879.

In the 1870s, San Francisco also passed another unusual law

called the Laundry Ordinance. It imposed a license fee of $2 every three months on laundries operating with one-horse vehicles, of $4 on those using two-horse vehicles, and of $15 on those using *no* horse-drawn vehicles. Since Chinese people were very much involved in the laundry business and normally carried clothes in baskets slung from poles, this ordinance seemed deliberately drawn up to discriminate against them.

In 1878 the United States Congress joined the anti-Chinese trend with its Fifteen Passenger Bill, which limited ships crossing the Pacific to no more than 15 Chinese passengers. President Rutherford B. Hayes refused to sign the bill, however, because it contradicted the terms of the Burlingame Treaty concluded with China 10 years earlier to encourage free exchange of the people of the two countries.

But this kind of restraint was not to last much longer. Repression and exclusion of Chinese labor were becoming hot political issues. Even politicians who had previously spoken approvingly of the industry of Chinese workers and the contribution they had made to the nation's growth now had to join the "Chinese must go" movement if they wanted to be reelected. A vote taken in California in 1879 produced 154,638 votes for Chinese exclusion and only 883 against. Since Chinese immigrants in the United States were not eligible for naturalization and citizenship, they had no voice in this or any other election.

2. *Exclusion of Chinese Immigrants*

In the early 1880s, the opposition to unlimited Chinese immigration reached its highest point. In Congress, Californians traded support with representatives of the Southern states, each group seeking the help needed to push through its own form of discriminatory legislation. A delegation of officials went to Peking and persuaded the Chinese government to alter the Burlingame Treaty to the extent that the United States could limit but not completely prohibit the immigration of Chinese laborers.

In 1882, Congress passed the Chinese Exclusion Act, which ended the free immigration to America of Chinese laborers, whether skilled or unskilled, for a period of 10 years. Later acts extended this period again and again until the law was finally repealed in 1943.

In 1888 the prohibition against Chinese immigration was reinforced with the even stiffer terms of the Scott Act. This law made it clear that exclusion applied to any Chinese worker, whether living in China or not, and prohibited the return to the United States of Chinese people temporarily out of the country, even if they had valid re-entry certificates. In this way some 20,000 Chinese laborers were cut off from their jobs, property, and families in the United States.

The Geary Act of 1892 went further. It extended the original Exclusion Act for another 10 years, denied Chinese people the right of bail in habeas corpus proceedings, and required all Chinese living in the United States to get certificates of registration within one year or else be subject to deportation.

The Chinese ambassador in Washington protested that the Geary Act was "in violation of every principle of justice, equity, and fair dealing between two friendly powers." The Chinese consul advised Chinese citizens in the United States not to register because he was sure the act would be struck down as unconstitutional. But despite the fact that it violated treaties with China, the Geary Act was upheld by the Supreme Court. Chief Justice Stephen Field said it was justified on grounds of public interest and necessity.

From that point onward Chinese people in the United States could be and were confronted at any time with demands to see their registration certificates. If unable to produce certificates they had to provide proof that they were legal residents or risk being sent back to China.

During this period Chinese officials, teachers, students, merchants, and travelers were still allowed to come to the United States, usually only for short periods of time and always with a fistful of documents authorizing their visit. Many of them had degrading experiences at the ports of entry, where they were harassed by immigration officials, treated with suspicion, and often questioned for a long time to make sure that their entry permits were authentic.

As word of these indignities got around, many of the educated Chinese people who were entitled to come to the United States began to stay away by choice. Moreover, thousands of Chinese living in America returned to China. Between 1890 and 1920, the number of Chinese people in the United States dropped from 107,000 to 61,000. A great many workers could not afford to give up their jobs, however, and had to stay on in this unhappy atmosphere. It became a risky business for them to make the usual visits back to their families in China because of the possibility that the immigration authorities would not accept their papers when they came back into the country. They were afraid, too, that the law might be changed yet again to keep them out permanently.

No one knows how much smuggling of immigrants went on during the period of exclusion but there is not much doubt that a good many Chinese people came into the country illegally. Trade routes for smugglers grew up in Cuba, Canada, and Mexico, and sometimes the charge was as high as $2,500 per person. In 1923 Canada and Mexico passed their own exclusion laws, which made these smuggling routes doubly dangerous.

Chinese brokers turned smuggling into a profitable business and built up good connections for forged papers in New York, San Francisco, and other ports of entry. The Attorney General's office estimated that three of the biggest racketeers dealing in forged Chinese passports made a profit of about $3 million a year.

Chinese men being jailed after an unsuccessful attempt to enter the United States illegally in 1934. They had been smuggled in from the island of Trinidad sewn into potato sacks.

In addition to smuggling, there were other illegal methods of avoiding the discriminatory restrictions on Chinese immigration. Several of these methods made use of the fact that anyone born in the United States was automatically an American citizen. His children, too, had United States citizenship, even though they had been born in another country. When the 1906 earthquake and fire in San Francisco destroyed the public records in Chinatown, many Chinese people took advantage of this opportunity to establish their citizenship. They declared themselves to have been born in the United States whether in fact they had been or not. If a man could tell his story convincingly enough, the authorities, lacking any written records, had no choice but to accept his word. He then had the right to bring his children into the country when they came of age.

When a Chinese who was an American citizen returned

from a visit to China, he would record with the immigration authorities the names of any children born to him since he had last entered the United States. During the period of restricted immigration, many so-called "paper sons" achieved citizenship through this system. Paper sons were not actual descendants of their paper fathers but were boys who wanted to get into the United States and had no legal means of doing so. Whatever interrogation the immigration authorities tried, it was almost impossible to tell the difference between genuine sons and paper sons. But life was complicated for a boy who came into the country in this way. All his official documents showed his name to be the same as that of his paper father, but in the Chinese community he was known by his own name.

In 1924, a new immigration law was passed which affected the Chinese, although it was not aimed at them directly. The Immigration Act of 1924 stipulated that aliens not eligible for United States citizenship—that is, all nonwhites except for people of African descent—should no longer be allowed to enter the country. In theory this act put an end to all Chinese immigration, but the earlier exclusion laws had already succeeded in cutting the flow of immigrants down to almost nothing. What the 1924 law did do was to prevent Chinese-born wives of Chinese-American citizens from coming to the United States. Up until this time, these women had usually been allowed to enter the country. The new ruling which prohibited their admission caused a great deal of hardship in the Chinese communities, where women were already scarce.

During the last half of the 19th century, when Chinese immigrants in the United States were suffering under various forms of persecution, the Chinese in the Hawaiian Islands were living in relative peace. From 1852 onward, many thousands of Chinese had come to the islands to work on the sugar plantations. When they had completed their five years of indentured labor

Honolulu Harbor in the 19th century. Honolulu was the main port of entry for Chinese people who came to the Hawaiian Islands during the 1850s to work on the sugar plantations.

on the plantations, most of the immigrants moved into the towns and worked as carpenters, cooks, waiters, mechanics, tailors, and gardeners. They also set up their own businesses—bakeries, restaurants, laundries, and shops. In later years many Chinese became industrialists, merchants, bankers, doctors, lawyers, and teachers.

During the years when Hawaii was an independent country, its government had passed immigration control laws which had never been enforced. However, when Hawaii became a United States territory in 1898, American exclusion laws and other acts restricting the freedom of the Chinese were extended to Hawaii.

3. *Repeal of the Exclusion Laws*

By the time that China and the United States were fighting together as allies in World War II, the old exclusion laws began to look a bit ridiculous. Chinese people in America made valuable contributions to the war effort. Because of the wartime shortage of labor, they had opportunities to work in jobs where they had not before been welcome. During these years they broke out of their Chinatown seclusion and grew to know and like their fellow Americans; in the same way their fellow Americans grew to know and like them.

The movement for the repeal of the Chinese exclusion laws was strengthened when Madame Chiang Kai-shek, wife of the leader of the Chinese Nationalist party, visited the United States in 1943. She had many friends in America from her schooldays at Wellesley College in Massachusetts. She also had all the persuasive powers of a beautiful woman. During her visit she held dinner parties for influential congressmen and addressed a joint session of Congress—the first woman ever invited to do so.

Madame Chiang Kai-shek's tour was a triumph, and it melted away most of the remaining resistance to giving Chinese people in America a new deal. Late in 1943, a bill was passed which abolished existing Chinese exclusion laws, provided for an annual quota of immigrants on the same basis as those from other countries, and gave Chinese people in the United States the same

Madame Chiang Kai-shek makes an appearance at Madison Square Garden in New York City during her tour of the United States in 1943. She is accompanied by Thomas E. Dewey, the governor of New York (left), and John D. Rockefeller, Jr. (right).

rights of naturalization as anyone else.

Immigration was still not easy, however. According to the quota system, the number of immigrants allowed to enter from any country was based on the number of people from that country who lived in the United States in the year 1920. (The calculation was made by taking one-sixth of one percent of this number.) However, because of the exclusion laws, there were relatively few Chinese in the States in 1920. After the 1943 bill was passed, the quota allowed for only 105 Chinese immigrants a year. There was also a separate quota for non-Chinese people coming from China.

Three years later, an amendment to the bill allowed the wives and children of Chinese Americans to enter the country as non-quota residents. Chinese wives of American citizens were also able to come to the United States under the provisions of the War Brides Act, passed in 1947. In 1952 the husbands and children of Chinese-American women were granted non-quota status.

Whatever opponents of the 1943 bill may have feared, there was no flood of immigrants from China. For the first eight years the quota was not fully taken up, and only after families were allowed to enter did people start arriving in any number. For a while immigrants were overwhelmingly female, beginning at last to balance out the large numbers of bachelors and men separated from their wives in Chinatowns everywhere. When the Communists took over in China in 1949, there was an exodus to the United States of people with relatives here and of merchants and former officials of the defeated Nationalist party.

In the early 1950s the United States Congress passed refugee relief acts to help cope with refugees from World War II and from the Communist regime in China; several thousand Chinese immigrants entered the country under the provisions of these acts. Also in the early '50s the United States consulate in China was closed down. From that time onward immigrants and refugees have been processed through the American consular offices in Hong Kong. In May 1962, Communist China suddenly allowed a flood of refugees to leave Kwangtung province and go to Hong Kong. The British administrators of that already desperately overcrowded island were appalled and tried to send them back. This caused a great outcry of compassion from Americans, and arrangements were made for 15,000 refugees to come to the United States between 1962 and 1965.

Gradually, over the years from 1965 to 1968, United States immigration laws were changed to abolish all national quotas. The total annual quota for immigrants from outside the Western Hemisphere was fixed at 170,000, with no more than 20,000 people to come in from any one country. In the first full year of the new plan, over 17,000 immigrants came in from Hong Kong and Formosa. Many more are arriving today. Quite a few of the immigrants are young people with experience in student activist demonstrations in Hong Kong, and they are bringing a new militancy to American Chinatowns.

Even with the new liberalism in immigration, visas are not easy to get. Applications are processed partly on a first-come, first-served basis but also on the basis of a complicated system of preferences. For instance, people who have close relatives in the United States, who are distinguished scientists and professors, or who have special skills which will benefit the United States get priority over others.

It takes intelligence and persistence to work through the maze of red tape that leads to the prize of an immigrant's visa. And in Hong Kong and Formosa, where the offices are swamped with applications, it takes money too—for bribes to get one's application noticed, or for lawyers to plead one's case. So although there are no longer any laws specifically discriminating against them, few poor Chinese laborers ever get accepted as immigrants.

PART IV

Chinatowns in America

1. *Home Away from Home*

Put yourself in the cloth slippers of a Chinese immigrant on his way to San Francisco in the 1850s. You are an energetic young man of 22, with a wife and three children whom you have left behind in Kwangtung province. You will be sending money home to support them and perhaps also to help your parents, who live nearby.

Life has always been a struggle in your village. As soon as you were big enough, you had to help with the chores of farming and the tasks required for day-to-day survival, so you have never had much time for education. But your parents taught you the Confucian principles of family loyalty and obedience. Each member of your family has a close concern for the welfare of all the others, and you know your wife and children will not be alone while you are away.

In the past two years you have seen how some neighbors have become unbelievably wealthy from the money and gold that their sons are sending back from California. So, after endless family councils, you decide to borrow money for the passage and go for a few years to this land of fabulous wealth. Perhaps you will be able to set your family on their feet and bring them the riches and prestige that no amount of hard work in Kwangtung seems likely ever to win.

You are already in strange territory when you go to Hong Kong to arrange the terms of a loan with the passage brokers. To your

On the docks of Hong Kong, Chinese immigrants prepare to board a ship bound for San Francisco, the big city of the Golden Mountains.

dismay, you have to borrow far more money than you had expected. But eventually the brokers put you safely on board a ship bound for San Francisco. Once you recover from the miseries of seasickness after the first few days, the voyage turns out to be fun. For the first time in your life you have no work to do, and you make friends among the other passengers who are going to California with the same high hopes as your own.

The day that your ship docks in Gum San Ta Foy, the big city of the Golden Mountains, you dress carefully in clean clothes to make the best possible impression and bundle up your few possessions. As you go down the gangplank you are nervous and excited.

Then to your horror, you are swamped by hordes of huge, hairy men wearing clothes which look as if they have not been washed for days. They are shouting at you, and you don't understand a word. They seem to be asking for money, and you can't remember what each coin is worth. Even when you straighten the money out, prices seem outrageously high. You are so confused you could weep, but you are determined to keep face in front of these Western barbarians. Somehow you have to find work and a place to sleep, but every time you ask for directions people look at you blankly or even start hooting with laughter. The friends who came over with you are as confused as you are.

Just when you are wishing that you had never come, you see six Chinese walking along the dock, pigtails swinging. You throw dignity to the winds and rush toward them. Several you cannot understand but one speaks your own dialect and tells you he comes from a village only 50 miles from yours. He explains that he and the others are representatives from the Six Chinese Companies, an organization representing the six districts in Kwangtung from which most immigrants come. They have houses in the Chinese Street where you can spend a few days, and they have contacts with people who can help you find work.

In the Chinese Street it is just like home. Everyone wears familiar clothes, speaks the various Chinese dialects, and eats Chinese food. You feel safe and at ease there.

In the 1850s and 60s, many immigrants like the one we have followed from Kwangtung made the long journey to the United States. The Chinese Street in San Francisco quickly grew into Little China, the early name for Chinatown. The pattern of settlement among the Chinese immigrants was just the same as that of other immigrant groups arriving in American ports during these years. Whether the newcomers were Chinese, Italian, Greek, Irish, German, Polish, or Scandinavian, they all tended to congregate with people of their own nationality. But the need for the security of an ethnic community was even stronger for the Chinese than for European immigrants. For them the culture shock of immigration was much more severe. Their appearance, language, dress, food, religion, and philosophy were entirely different from those of the majority of Americans. For the Chinese, Chinatown provided a home away from home where the way of life was familiar and reassuring. Later, when the mobs were out to get them, Chinese people also needed the safety of their Chinatowns for sheer survival.

Wherever Chinese people congregated, someone would eventually open a grocery store and import familiar foods from home. The store would become a meeting place, a sort of club, to which a restaurant might be added. Tables for popular Chinese games such as fan-tan and mah-jong would be set out on Sundays. There might be a shrine in a building nearby; then bunkhouses and dormitories would be established, and perhaps an opium den.

Gradually the immigrant community developed within the same formal patterns that existed in China. A fong would be opened—a room where people from the same locality in China

Sam Fong's grocery store on Clay Street in San Francisco, 1908. In many Chinese communities, stores such as this not only sold food imported from China but also served as meeting places for the immigrants.

would come to gossip and to play cards. They could also sleep and eat there when they were out of work or visiting from another town. The fong could be used as a mailing address, and people could pay into and borrow money from its cooperative bank.

Family associations were also set up in the Chinese immigrant community. In all China there were only 438 different family names, and people felt a kinship with those who had the same name as their own. Family associations in the United States provided a room and food for the immigrants, if needed. They paid the funeral expenses for any of their members who had no immediate family in the United States. Often they made arrangements for bones of the deceased to be shipped home to their families in China. The associations provided interpreters, settled quarrels, and organized the celebrations for important festivals like New Year. Expenses were covered by charging dues to members.

As the number of Chinese immigrants in the United States grew, Chinese people had a tendency to move to cities where there were settlements of other immigrants with the same family name. Eventually, certain families came to predominate in certain cities. Thus today in Phoenix the Chinese community is dominated by Oongs, in Pittsburgh by Yees, in Washington and Honolulu by Lees, in Chicago by Moys, and in Sacramento by Fongs.

Chinese people who found no one of the same name in the area where they settled could join district associations, in which immigrants from the same districts in China banded together for their mutual welfare. Or the immigrants could belong to several kinds of associations at the same time.

All of these organizations sent representatives to the so-called Chinese benevolent associations, which had great influence in the Chinatowns, acting as unofficial governments and spokesmen for the Chinese communities. The benevolent associations were often known by different names in different cities. The one in Honolulu was called the United Chinese Society. In San Francisco the Chinese Six Companies, which had started out as a combination of six district associations, assumed the functions and characteristics of a benevolent association, while still keeping its old name.

2. *The Big City of the Golden Mountains*

By 1870, more than 20 years after the gold rush had begun, 99 percent of all Chinese in the United States were living west of the Rocky Mountains. Most of them came in through the port of San Francisco, and the Chinatown in this city grew rapidly. At first its population fluctuated considerably, changing with the seasons. In winter unemployment brought the fish cutters in from the northern salmon canneries, the farm laborers in from the Sacramento River delta, and the gold washers in from the mountains, where winter snow had made their work impossible. But when the gold mines were exhausted, the railroad finished, and rural areas hit by the 1870 depression, thousands of families sought refuge in Chinatown. Then it became desperately overcrowded the year round.

The community's boundaries were limited by the San Francisco City Board of Supervisors to an area seven blocks long by three blocks wide. Other citizens of the city, supported by the newspapers, protested vigorously if the Chinese tried to extend these boundaries. So the inhabitants of Chinatown had to create extra accommodations as best they could. They added sheds, lean-tos, booths, and balconies to existing buildings. They burrowed three stories underground and made connecting passages and cellars. (Before the earthquake destroyed these old buildings, it was said that one could pass right through Chinatown below ground level.)

Chinatown could meet the needs of its people, from birth to

Chinese immigrants dictate messages to a public letter writer in Chinatown. Chinese people living in the United States maintained close contact with their families in China.

death, in a style almost identical to that existing back home in Kwangtung. In addition to the meeting houses of the various associations, the community had Chinese theaters, restaurants, gambling halls, opium parlors, schools, temples, banks, import-export houses, clothing, cigar, and shoe factories, laundries, and retail stores—all owned by Chinese, staffed by Chinese employees, and serving Chinese customers.

The population was mostly male—in 1885 there were 14,500 bunks for single men in Chinatown. As the merchants of the community prospered, however, they brought their wives over from China, married Chinese women by proxy, or obtained brides from dealers who smuggled girls in or even bought them from impoverished Chinese families. Family life in Chinatown was quiet. A respectable woman rarely went out of doors but was publicly honored once every seven years during the Good

Lady Festival. Then women put on beautiful clothes stored in cedarwood chests for just this occasion and became the center of attention in all the processions and celebrations.

The liveliest festival of all was that held at the Chinese New Year. It was, and still is, celebrated in American Chinatowns just as it was in China. Festivities lasted for a week and included parades, lion dances, exploding firecrackers, banquets in restaurants, historical plays accompanied by drums, cymbals, and gongs, and prayers in the temples.

But for all its color and excitement, Chinatown was in reality a ghetto—an overcrowded slum. The community had many of the social problems common to ghettos everywhere. Crime and vice —gambling, drugs, prostitution, blackmail—flourished, often under the protection and encouragement of the tongs, secret brotherhoods which had originated in China. In Chinatown's criminal underworld, professional killers known as highbinders could be hired to commit murder for a price. Yet these same men were also the formal and recognized agents of justice for the Chinese authorities. It was impossible for San Francisco city police to enforce city law in Chinatown, so they left the community to govern itself.

At times things got out of hand. Wars between the tong brotherhoods, which were frequent in China, broke out in American Chinatowns and brought disgrace and dishonor to law-abiding Chinese people. Lurid stories of the viciousness of tong warfare survived long after the wars themselves ended. (The last known battle between tongs was in 1931.)

On the whole, the elaborate organization and control of Chinese life made self-government in Chinatown work, despite the enormous problems of crime and overcrowding. The Chinese Six Companies, the unofficial government of the community, worked hard to settle arguments, stimulate trade, and promote the welfare of the Chinese people in America.

Chinatown after the earthquake and fire in 1906

3. *The Earth Dragon Trembles*

On April 18, 1906, a little after five o'clock in the morning, the earth beneath San Francisco shook. Buildings trembled and collapsed, cobblestone pavements cracked and opened up, streets sank, walls and chimneys crashed to the ground. Shock after shock of a massive earthquake roared through the city, moving the land on the west side of the San Andreas fault 16 feet north of where it had been before.

All through San Francisco, people grabbed their most precious belongings and fled into the streets rather than risk being crushed to death inside the buildings. But then fire broke out. Lamps and stoves had been overturned, gas mains fractured, and electric wiring wrenched apart. Flames swept the city, and by nightfall the whole of Chinatown was on fire. People swarmed out of the area, carrying bundles on poles. Martial law had been declared, and some of the inhabitants of Chinatown had to be forced to leave their homes and businesses at bayonet point. Eventually all were evacuated to a park in North Beach. Later they were moved to the Presidio, an army post in the northwestern part of the city.

Long after the earthquake was over, the fires continued to burn. Water mains were broken, and firefighters had little chance of controlling the flames. Dynamite was used to clear firebreaks but in spite of every effort the fire blazed for three days.

The earthquake took place at a time when anti-Chinese feeling was still strong in San Francisco, and Chinatown's inhabitants felt very insecure removed from their familiar seclusion. They were so conditioned to expect ill treatment from white people that they were afraid the relief services would not feed them. They did experience some hostility but generally received the help that they needed.

When the danger was over, a whole city was waiting to be rebuilt. The Chinese had plenty of offers for their valuable land in Chinatown, but they would not sell. Instead they set to work rebuilding their homes and businesses. For many of the Chinese in San Francisco this was a turning point. With the reconstruction of Chinatown they began to look upon themselves as settlers in the United States rather than visiting foreigners.

4. *Rebuilding in San Francisco*

The new Chinatown was a lot less colorful and exotic than the old one had been but it was a lot less squalid too. Bright street lights replaced the dim glow of Chinese lanterns. Movie houses replaced the classical Chinese theaters. Stores used cash registers to supplement the abacus, the traditional Chinese counting device. Shops sold mass-produced goods side by side with hand-made works of oriental art. Private family dwellings were built to take the place of the old crowded dormitories.

Many of the changes in the new Chinatown would have come eventually, with the changing times, but the destruction and rebuilding after the earthquake hurried them along. The spirit of revolution in China itself was spreading its influence too. When the Manchu dynasty was overthrown in 1911, and with it the old Confucian principles, men throughout Chinatown cut off their queues and replaced their robes with modern American clothes.

Some of the rebuilding in Chinatown was planned to develop the tourist potential of the community. Elegant Chinese restaurants were built for the white people who were attracted by the foreign feeling of Chinatown now that it had been cleaned up. Nightclubs with Chinese entertainers became popular too. The tourist attractions of Chinatown have continued to provide useful extra business for the community.

Temples were rebuilt so that immigrants could practice their own blend of Buddhism and Taoism, based on the worship of many different gods and goddesses. In the temples were painted statues of the gods, each in its own carved and decorated shrine, bronze vases and urns, gongs, incense burners, scrolls of Chinese script, elaborate teakwood tables, and silken embroideries. About 20 of these temples remain in California today but most of them are tourist attractions and are not greatly used by Chinese people.

The Christian churches had missionaries in the new Chinatown. They taught English, acted as spokesmen, tried to protect people from violence, and worked untiringly to rescue girls from prostitution. Today many people in Chinatown belong to the Christian churches, which attract young people with a wide range of activities, such as classes in Mandarin (the most common

Sightseers stroll along Grant Avenue, the main street of San Francisco's Chinatown. Today, as in the past, the foreign atmosphere of Chinatown attracts thousands of tourists each year.

dialect of the Chinese language), classical Chinese literature, Western drama, and dancing.

Family and district associations continued as before, but in the 20th century their strongest appeal was to first-generation immigrants who needed the comfort and reassurance of familiar organizations as well as their practical help. American-born Chinese citizens began to use the social services provided by the United States government instead of relying on the old immigrant organizations. Even the tongs slowly transformed themselves, changing their names to merchants associations or Chinese freemason organizations and taking up charitable work.

The Chinese benevolent association—the Six Companies—continued to be the supreme authority in the new Chinatown. It brought together representatives from all the other organizations, including chambers of commerce, women's clubs, schools, newspapers, even seamen's unions. The association preserved the old tradition requiring that every alternate term its president be someone whose family came from Toishan, reflecting the predominance of people from that area. Today the benevolent association's influence is not as strong as it once was, but the organization still plays an important role in Chinatown. Among other activities, it organizes the traditional celebrations like China's Independence Day parades and the Chinese New Year.

Modern Chinatown in San Francisco preserves many of the features of earlier periods, but the process of change has continued. Until quite recently the community had its own telephone exchange with the directory printed in Chinese. This is now a

A golden dragon leads the New Year's parade in San Francisco's Chinatown. The annual celebration of the Chinese New Year is a tradition from the past which has been preserved in the modern Chinese community.

thing of the past. Some of the institutions of Chinatown have successfully combined the traditional and the modern. The Tung-Wah hospital, staffed entirely by Chinese doctors and nurses, uses the latest international medical techniques but also some of the ancient herbal remedies. It is popular, too, because it serves Chinese food.

Family ties in Chinatown are still strong but the old subservience to senior members of the family is changing. In her book *Fifth Chinese Daughter*, Jade Snow Wong, a Chinese-American writer, describes the conflicts of growing up torn between the customs of the ancient culture, which controlled her parents' lives, and the modern American culture, which she saw among her classmates at school. Another San Francisco writer, Pardee Lowe, tells how life at home was filled with polite salutations and formal bowings and scrapings. "For the most part all this bored us," he says, "and we longed to escape from it and do as our American school friends did."

The San Francisco Chinatown which early in the century seemed shining and new has gradually become old and run-down. Housing is far below the acceptable standards of the present day, and living conditions are unhealthy. San Francisco city authorities have rated 82 percent of Chinatown's dwellings as substandard, compared with 20 percent for the rest of the city. The tuberculosis rate in Chinatown is three times that of the rest of San Francisco. Population density is higher than anywhere in the United States except Manhattan. The colorful streets of Chinatown are still popular with tourists but the exotic exteriors of the buildings hide a super slum.

5. *Chinatowns in Other American Cities*

Other Chinatowns grew up throughout the United States in much the same way as did the one in San Francisco. Immigrants went wherever there was a demand for labor. In places where many Chinese immigrants settled, Chinatowns appeared. Some were short lived, disappearing when the industry that produced them dwindled away. Such was the fate of the Chinatowns in the mining and railroad communities of Butte, Montana, Rock Springs, Wyoming, and Denver, Colorado. Others remained and prospered.

Today, 39 percent of the Chinese people in the United States live in California, 18 percent in New York, and 12 percent in Hawaii. The remaining 31 percent are scattered around the country, with at least some in every state in the Union. Less than half of these people live in Chinatowns; increasing numbers are moving to the suburbs and integrating with larger American communities. Some cities have such a small Chinese population that their needs are met by just two or three stores, a couple of restaurants, and an association meeting room.

Some Chinatowns have become victims of urban progress. The old Chinatown in Honolulu was torn down to make room for a new cultural center. Pittsburgh's Chinatown was destroyed so that a new expressway could be built. Philadelphia's is a pale shadow of its former self since road building and slum clearance have whittled it away.

Despite all these changes, there are still substantial Chinatowns in New York, Honolulu, Los Angeles, Sacramento, Chicago, Boston, Seattle, Washington, D.C., and, of course, San Francisco.

At one time or another, Los Angeles has had four Chinatowns. In 1909, Lonie Quan started a colony on the site of what became in 1931 the union depot. A portion of the old town still remains today. Another community grew up along North Spring Street, and in 1938 two new Chinatowns were built as planned projects, as much to attract tourists as to house Chinese people. One of these was China City, established by Mrs. Christine Sterling. This Chinatown looks a bit like a movie set, with its souvenir shops and restaurants built around a central plaza. Peter Soo Hoo

A funeral procession on Mott Street in New York City's Chinatown during the early years of the 20th century

was the moving spirit behind the other Chinatown, which is on Broadway at College Street. It is controlled by an all-Chinese corporation which owns half the lots. The area has many two-story buildings on broad open streets lit with brilliant neon lights. Chinatowns are sharing in the population boom in Los Angeles, and their populations are increasing too.

The first Chinese resident of New York City is said to have been Pung Hua Wing Ching, who came there as a servant in 1807. By 1869 small groups of Chinese people were beginning to drift in from the West Coast, and in the next few years Chinatown really got going. By 1887 it had about 1,000 inhabitants, mostly men. In the 1920s, New York's Chinatown shared San Francisco's troubles with tong warfare, gambling, and drugs, but now it has less crime and juvenile delinquency than most other ethnic quarters in New York.

Many of the buildings in this Chinatown are old and overcrowded, in one of the poorest parts of Manhattan. For a long time little new construction took place. But now new apartment buildings are being completed, some of them reaching out beyond the confines of the old Chinatown area. In 1952 the Chinese Merchants Association built its first multistory commercial project, which included a Chinese community center with an auditorium, gymnasium, offices, and a Chinese school.

On holidays and Sundays, Chinese Americans come to Chinatown from all around New York City and from the suburbs of New York, New Jersey, and Connecticut. They come to have a meal, meet friends and relatives, play mah-jong, and collect letters from Hong Kong and Formosa, the only remaining parts of "home" with which they have regular contact.

6. *The Decline and Rise of American Chinatowns*

For a while it looked as though American Chinatowns might wither away completely. Changes had begun to take place which made their continued existence doubtful. Young Chinese people growing up in the United States were rebelling against the restrictions on their freedom of the old-style family traditions. Today that rebellion continues. Most young Chinese are just not interested in perpetuating the ancient Chinese culture in their day-to-day lives. They are impatient with the old formality. They grow up speaking a different language from that spoken by the elders of the family, and they go to American schools, where they rapidly absorb a contemporary pattern of life.

Chinese families have made sacrifices to make sure that their children get a good education, and large numbers of them go on to college. They are trained for much better jobs than those Chinatown has to offer, and they enter the professions alongside other Americans with similar educations. There is little discrimination now against educated Americans of Chinese ancestry; they are free to live and work wherever they wish. More and more they are marrying across racial barriers, although this is still not general. In fact, until recently, 12 states—Arizona, Georgia, Idaho, Louisiana, Mississippi, Missouri, Nebraska, Nevada, South Dakota, Utah, Virginia, and Wyoming—had laws forbidding Orientals from marrying whites. These laws were struck down by a Supreme Court ruling in 1967. Similar laws had been repealed in California in 1948, in Oregon in 1951, and in Montana in 1953.

Other changes have affected the way of life preserved in Chinatown. Better education and job opportunities have made Chinese girls less likely to accept their traditional role of confinement to the home. They have learned to make decisions for themselves and to become independent of the crutch of Chinatown.

The traditional Chinatown organizations have also been affected. Splinter groups have broken away from the Chinese associations in an attempt to emphasize the American heritage of Chinese Americans. One is the Chinese American Citizens Alliance, which defends the rights and privileges of its members and fights segregation and discrimination. In the larger cities most of its board members are college graduates.

All of these developments seemed to be hastening the decline of the Chinatowns in American cities. In 1940 there were 28 cities in the United States with Chinatowns. Fifteen years later there were only 16. With so few new immigrants coming into the country, further decline seemed certain, as second- and third-generation Chinese Americans continued to move into the mainstream of American life.

Then the revisions of the immigration laws which took place from 1965 to 1968 altered the picture completely. Even though the new immigrants coming in from Hong Kong are already partly Westernized, they still welcome the homelike atmosphere of Chinatown. A period spent in the Chinese community breaks people in gently and provides a good jumping-off ground. Living is cheap there and jobs are available. Professional people coming into the country often accept menial jobs in Chinatown while they are getting on their feet.

Living conditions in Chinatown are also improving. Recent nondiscrimination laws make it possible for Chinese Americans to buy land as it becomes available, so they can extend the boundaries of Chinatown and put up new buildings. Now the populations of the Chinatowns in San Francisco, New York, and Los Angeles are growing again. (Since 1965, the population of San Francisco's Chinatown has nearly doubled.) There is still a strong suggestion of the ghetto about these communities, but they are also places that Chinese Americans feel sentimentally attached to. Family groups from all social levels go into Chinatown to attend weddings, festivals, and funerals, and to patronize restaurants and grocery stores.

There is a new militancy in Chinatown too. In San Francisco a group of young people from Hong Kong have formed a militant organization called the China Youth. Other young people who call themselves Red Guards take the Black Panthers as their model. They are in revolt against their elders in the Chinese-American communities and also against white people, whom they call honkies. The Red Guards are scandalizing older Chinese people by hissing "Off the honkies" to white tourists on the streets of Chinatown.

The new militancy in San Francisco's Chinatown and the renewal of community life there have also found expression, strangely enough, in Chinese resistance to school busing. In 1971, many parents in Chinatown refused to let their children participate in a busing program which would have taken them out of the local public schools, where enrollment is 90 percent Chinese. The reason for their opposition, they said, was simple: they did not want their children to attend schools in which they would be a

A Chinese-American woman protests the busing of school children during a meeting between parents and the San Francisco Board of Education, July 1971.

racial and cultural minority, cut off from the Chinese community. A boycott of the public schools was put into effect, and many Chinatown youngsters were transferred to private Chinese schools, which had previously held after-school classes in Chinese language and culture.

Other developments in Chinatown indicate a new mood of change in the Chinese-American community. Chinatown's political sympathies have traditionally been with Chiang Kai-shek and the Nationalists, even after the party's many years of exile in Formosa. But there is a gradual shift now toward interest in the Chinese mainland and Mao Tse-tung. Chinese Americans have begun to respect the efforts the communists are making to improve the quality of life in China. They have also no doubt been influenced by the renewed contact between mainland China and the United States which took place in the early 1970s. Whatever the cause, Mao Tse-tung's "Little Red Book" is becoming a best seller in American Chinatowns.

PART V

Changing Attitudes toward Chinese Americans

Americans of Chinese ancestry are a tiny .2 percent of the total population. Thousands of people in the United States have never met any one of them. Yet most Americans, if asked, could tell you what Chinese people are like. We all carry around a rag-bag of preconceived ideas about different groups of people. Just mention Jews, students, Black Panthers, Olympic skiers— or Chinese—and an instant stereotype pops into our minds, constructed out of scores of impressions received from various sources throughout our lives. The truth is, of course, that any two Chinese Americans are as different from each other as you are from your next-door neighbor. But we do develop certain attitudes about groups, and those about Chinese people and Americans of Chinese ancestry have gone through some radical changes over the years.

1. *Social, Political, and Economic Pressures*

Often the attitudes of other Americans toward the Chinese have changed in response to changing economic conditions. During the early days in California, the majority of Chinese immigrants were laborers, and attitudes toward them improved or worsened in relation to the need for labor. At first employers valued them for their diligence, dependability, and obedience. White fellow workers sometimes mocked the Chinese for their racial differences, but while there were jobs for everyone, they

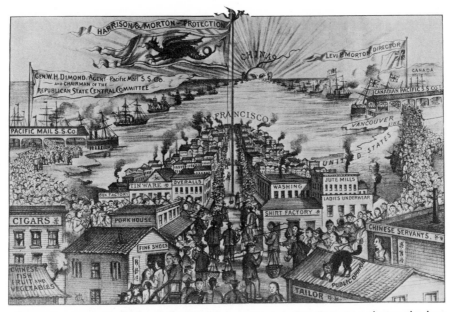

A cartoon portraying Chinese immigrants pouring into San Francisco during the last half of the 19th century. The artist expressed the fears of many Americans who believed that the Chinese were flooding the job market and shutting out white labor.

treated them with toleration, showing no real malice. With the depression of the 1870s, however, attitudes of indifference changed to violent persecution and to the "Chinese must go" campaign of the Workingman's Party.

Politicians and newspapers followed the same swing. In 1852, when Chinese laborers joined the parades held to celebrate California's becoming the 31st state, the *Daily Alta California* wrote: "The China boys will yet vote at the same polls, study at the same schools and bow at the same altar as our countrymen." But from 1869 onward, after the completion of the railroad, newspapers and politicians took the part of the white majority. They accused the Chinese of lowering standards of living, shutting out white labor, and being criminal, secretive, corrupt, overly submissive, and deceitful. The same people who were once "Crocker's Pets" had become the "mongolian menace."

Attitudes toward the Chinese remained generally unfavorable until the period of World War II, when they began to change again under the influence of changing historical conditions. Chinese Americans fought and worked alongside other Americans and were accepted as "brave," "patient," "staunch," and "heroic." Some of this approval probably spilled over from the comradeship felt with China, who was a wartime ally of the United States.

During the Korean War, another change of attitude seemed likely. China was on the opposite side in this conflict, and American newspapers were calling the Chinese communists "heartless murderers" and "fighting hordes." Americans of Chinese ancestry were afraid that they might be interned, as Japanese Americans had been during World War II. So they demonstrated their loyalty by organizing anticommunist groups and declaring their support for the Chinese Nationalists on Formosa. There was some violence—for instance, a restaurant in San Francisco's Chinatown was attacked—but race relations committees managed to cool things down.

As long as Chinese Americans were living in tightly segregated Chinatowns, attitudes toward the Chinese in China tended to overlap with attitudes toward the Chinese in the United States. Then the communist take-over of China in the 1940s and the Korean War pushed China and the United States farther apart. At the same time, the steady integration of Chinese Americans into the community outside Chinatown brought them closer to their American neighbors. Firsthand knowledge began to replace stereotyped images of Chinese people in the minds of other Americans. Another factor influencing attitudes toward Chinese Americans in recent years was the civil rights movement of the 1960s, which made expressions of racial prejudice unfashionable and unacceptable among thinking people.

2. Influence of Newspapers, Movies, and Books

Our attitudes about groups of people are influenced not only by what happens in the world around us but also by the newspapers and books we read and the movies we see. American attitudes toward the Chinese have often been influenced by these sources. During the "Chinese must go" campaign of the 1870s, many newspapers seized the chance to boost their circulations by making headline news out of popular prejudices. The *San Francisco Chronicle* was looking for a cause which would attract new readers at the time when Denis Kearney was forming his Workingman's Party. The newspaper polished up Kearney's anti-Chinese speeches for him, reported them enthusiastically, and built him up into a champion of the "downtrodden working man." Some people believe that without the support of the *Chronicle*, Kearney would have remained a little-known rabble-rouser with none of the influence he later acquired.

To journalists in later periods, the Chinese, whether they lived in China or in American Chinatowns, became a source of colorful fill-ins whenever there was a scarcity of hard news. Yet many "eye-witness" reports about exotic events in Chinatown were written without the journalist's ever leaving his desk.

Some interesting studies have been made of newspaper and magazine articles written about Chinese people during various periods of time. Dr. Rose Hum Lee, in her book on the Chinese in the United States, reports the results of one such study, which examined periodicals published from 1919 to 1925. The majority of the articles about the Chinese dwelt on their "peculiarities," telling how they ate rats and snakes, did things backwards, ate soup with chopsticks, were all cunning, crafty, mysterious, and inscrutable, never said what they meant, and so on. About 21 percent of the articles from this period discussed Chinese students or the cultural contributions of the Chinese to art, theater, food, and philosophy. Another 25 percent described the efforts of Christian missionaries in China.

From 1925 to 1932 there was an increasing number of articles about assimilation; another popular topic during these years was the way in which the Chinese community provided its own welfare and relief services during the depression. Dr. Lee calls the years from 1937 to 1945 the heroic Chinese era, when American newspapers and magazines reflected the sympathy felt for China's fight against the invading Japanese. It was at this time, too, that Madame Chiang Kai-shek was doing such a good public relations job for China.

Americans have not only been influenced by what they read about the Chinese, but they have also been strongly affected by the images they see on the motion picture screen. During the 1920s, when most Chinese Americans lived apart from the mainstream of American life, moviemakers were producing their own melodramatic versions of what Chinatown and the Chinese people were like. The central figure in a whole series of cheap silent films set in Chinatown was Fu Manchu, an evil mandarin. He was cunning, treacherous, a murderer, and an opium eater. He carried a dagger tucked into the sleeve of his silk brocade gown and dropped poison into tea cups. He preyed on helpless females, especially if they were beautiful and white. In films like *Dragon's Claws* and *Mandarin Lover*, Fu Manchu smuggled white slaves into the United States in bales of tea. In others he was pictured selling drugs to millionaires in Chinatown restaurants.

A whole generation of Americans had their attitudes toward the Chinese shaped by Fu Manchu, with his hypnotic slanted eyes and long, graceful hands with clawlike fingernails. Until the mid-1930s most Chinese characters in American movies were either villains like Fu Manchu, slave girls, domestic servants, or hatchet-men associated with the tong secret brotherhoods. Later movies introduced the "wise" Chinese character like Charlie Chan, the Honolulu detective; however, Charlie was portrayed on the

The sinister movie villain Fu Manchu strongly influenced American attitudes toward the Chinese in the 1920s and 1930s.

screen as more quaint and clever than particularly intelligent. Then came the sexy, exotic ladies like Anna May Wong, a popular actress of Chinese ancestry, and films like *Shanghai Express*, in which Marlene Dietrich played a not very convincing Shanghai Lily.

Of course, Shanghai Lily, Charlie Chan, Fu Manchu, and the other stereotyped Chinese characters in the movies of the 1920s and 30s had very little similarity to real Chinese people. There were, however, other portrayals of Chinese characters which were more accurate and more sympathetic. Pearl Buck, who grew up in China as the daughter of a missionary, wrote about the Chinese with understanding and compassion. In *The Good Earth*, published in 1931, she gave vivid descriptions of the life of a peasant and his wife in China struggling to survive war, famine, flood, and poverty. This novel and *Dragon Seed*, another of her books about the Chinese, were made into films which became very popular in the United States. They did a lot to win American sympathy for Chinese people everywhere.

Henry R. Luce, the publisher of *Time*, *Life*, and *Fortune* magazines, was also a sinophile, that is, a lover of China. He too grew up there, the son of a missionary, and developed an affection for the Chinese which was often reflected in his publications.

3. *Chinoiserie in America*

American attitudes toward the Chinese people have gone through some radical changes over the years, but Chinese art and other aspects of Chinese culture have been consistently popular in the United States. In the 18th century, fashionable householders on the East Coast took great pride in their teakwood chests, lacquered tables, and delicate works of oriental art. These exotic imports were brought to the United States by sailing ships trading with China through Canton. They added just the right

A lacquerware sewing cabinet imported from China in the 19th century. It is equipped with sewing implements made of ivory. On the lid is a view of the harbor at Macao.

touch of refinement to the homes of people who wanted to lift their status a little above that of the rugged and practical pioneers.

Since the 18th century, American interest in Chinese art has remained high. Museums and art galleries all around the country have fine bronzes, scroll paintings, porcelain figures, wood carvings, and jade ornaments from ancient China, some of them dating back many hundreds of years before Christ. Philadelphia had a complete Chinese museum as early as 1839; its collection included costumes, street scenes, and displays of farming and manufacturing.

The growth of suburbs around American cities in the 1930s coincided with a renewed interest in *chinoiserie*, or things Chinese. This new Chinese craze probably came as a result of the Bowl of Rice benefits that were being held by Chinese-American women to raise money for the China Relief organization and to help children orphaned by the conflict in China.

Soft Chinese watercolors, pictures painted or embroidered on silk, Chinese figurines, colorful ginger jars, statuettes of Buddha, reproductions of Ming horses, paper fans, and all kinds of beautiful things, both mass-produced and handcrafted, decorated the walls and coffee tables of American homes in suburbia. People sipped tea from willow-patterned porcelain. Women wore silk party dresses with high mandarin collars. Families played mah-jong together. Although the principles of this game are much the same of those of gin rummy, the click-clack of the tiles and the exotic names of some of the pieces gave it a special attraction. Today many families still have a mah-jong set tucked away somewhere in the recreation room.

In the early 1970s, there were signs of another renewal of interest in things Chinese, no doubt in response to the improved relationship between China and the United States. In 1972, the year that President Nixon visited China, department stores were selling Mao suits and quilted Chinese coats to well-dressed

Americans of many ethnic origins enjoy Chinese food. Howard Wong's in Minneapolis, Minnesota, is one of the numerous restaurants throughout the United States which specialize in the Chinese cuisine.

Americans. Fashionable women were having their hair styled in China-doll bobs and making themselves up to look like Anna May Wong, the Chinese-American movie star of the 1920s and '30s.

Chinese restaurants have always been popular in the United States ever since the first ones were opened in San Francisco during the gold rush. The two dishes most often ordered are chow mein, which is meat or fish with bean sprouts and onions served with crisp noodles, and chop suey, a mixture of meat and vegetables with rice. Both are unknown in China and are rarely eaten by Chinese Americans but have become popular with Americans who have not yet learned to pick their way through unfamiliar menus in Chinese restaurants. As more people travel to the Orient and American taste in food becomes more sophisticated, the authentic Chinese dishes are becoming increasingly popular.

PART VI

Individual Achievements

1. *Above-Average Jobs*

Since there are only 435,000 Chinese Americans in the United States out of a total population of over 200 million, one would not expect to find them widely represented in the front ranks of business and the professions. But in fact, many Americans of Chinese ancestry do hold such important and influential positions. As a group, Chinese Americans have quietly and persistently moved so far from their earlier occupations as low-paid laborers that their average income is now higher than the national average.

A larger percentage of Chinese Americans graduate from college and go on to do postgraduate work than their white counterparts: 12 percent of Chinese Americans complete three years of college, and 14.5 percent complete four years or more, compared to 9 percent and 5.6 percent of white Americans. Naturally enough, this educational record leads to a high proportion of good jobs. Recent census figures show that 17.9 percent of the Chinese-American population hold professional and technical jobs, compared to 12 percent of white Americans. Throughout the country, Americans of Chinese ancestry are distinguishing themselves as teachers, architects, doctors, lawyers, dentists, research scientists, bankers, and businessmen.

Most of this achievement has taken place in the last 30 years or so, when the Chinese really began to enter the mainstream of American life. Until 1943, Chinese people had no way of acquiring United States naturalization. They were American citizens only if they had been born in this country or if their fathers had been born here. Lack of citizenship is a real handicap in the job market. Many of the jobs in the government offices of states, counties, and cities are open only to American citizens. Until very recently attorneys had to be citizens. In many states physicians still must meet this requirement. In a few states there have been laws stipulating that even barbers, guides, peddlers, plumbers, and chauffeurs must be citizens. In Colorado a waitress, janitor, or dishwasher working in a place that sells liquor must be a United States citizen.

With each new generation, more Chinese people have American citizenship by right of birth. Moreover, naturalization is now open to Chinese immigrants as it is to those of other nationalities. Young people are getting better and better educations. All this means that there are now more job opportunities for Chinese Americans than ever before, and increasingly they are turning up in the top jobs.

2. Government Officials

The first American of Chinese ancestry to sit in the United States Senate was Hiram L. Fong, who was elected to the Senate by the state of Hawaii in 1959. He was the first senator to represent Hawaii after it was admitted to the Union.

Mr. Fong was born in 1907, the 7th of 11 children; his parents had come to Hawaii in 1872 to work on the sugar plantations. When the boy Hiram was only four years old, he started to work, picking beans for cattle feed. Later he shined shoes, sold newspapers, caught and sold fish, and caddied on a golf course. He worked in order to save up enough money for each stage of his education. Three years after graduating from high school he had saved enough to enroll at the University of Hawaii, where he squeezed four years' work into three years and graduated with

United States Senator **Hiram L. Fong**

honors. Another two years of working and saving gave him enough to go on to Harvard Law School. He received his law degree in 1935 and set up a law office in Honolulu. Then in 1938 he was elected to the legislature of Hawaii, while the islands were still a United States territory. He served in the territorial legislature for 14 years. From 1959 to the present, Mr. Fong has represented the state of Hawaii in the United States Senate. He also finds time to oversee his varied business interests in the islands.

Another political figure, Wing F. Ong, was one of the first Chinese Americans to hold political office in a state government. In 1946 he was elected to the Arizona state legislature, where he served for five years.

Wing Ong was born in China, the son of a poor family. At the age of 13, Wing discovered that his father's birthplace had been California and that therefore he himself had the right to claim American citizenship. He came to California in 1921 and later moved to Phoenix, Arizona.

Wing Ong worked his way through grade school, high school, and college, often completing his studies in less than the usual time. At 32, he took a degree in law at the University of Arizona, graduating with honors. Three years later he was elected to the Arizona state legislature by a predominantly white electorate: there were only 13 voters of Chinese ancestry in his constituency.

3. *Businessmen*

Many Chinese Americans have put their talents to good use in the fields of business and finance. One of the earliest Chinese success stories is that of Joe Shoong, an immigrant who started his business career working for $30 a month in a shirt factory. Later he founded the chain of National Dollar Stores and the National Shoe Company, and by 1939 he had the second highest income in the state of California.

In the complicated world of high finance, a Chinese American,

Gerald Tsai, Jr.

Gerald Tsai, Jr., has been remarkably successful. Tsai is the founder and president of the Manhattan Fund, a mutual investment company with assets of more than $400 million. Born of a well-to-do family in Shanghai in 1928, Tsai came to the United States when he was 18 years old. After taking a bachelor's and a master's degree in economics at Boston University, he embarked on a career as an investment manager. Fourteen years later, Gerald Tsai had become one of the most influential men on Wall Street.

Another well-known Chinese-American businessman is C. Y. Tung, an industrialist and shipping magnate. He heads a group of shipping companies which operate out of Taiwan, Hong Kong, and New York, and is considered by many to be the largest individual shipowner in the world. In 1970, Mr. Tung paid $3.2 million for the ocean liner *Queen Elizabeth*, which he planned to turn into a floating university to be anchored in Hong Kong harbor. Unfortunately, a disastrous fire destroyed the famous old ship in 1972.

4. *Artists and Craftsmen*

Chinese culture has always been noted for the beauty of its art and the skill of its craftsmanship. Therefore it is not surprising that many Americans of Chinese ancestry have distinguished themselves as artists in various fields.

The style and technique of Chinese painting is quite different from that of the Western world. Yet artist Dong Kingman has combined the two traditions so successfully that his paintings have been exhibited in more than 40 museums and art galleries in the United States, including New York's Metropolitan Museum of Art.

Mr. Kingman was born in Oakland, California, in 1911, the son of a struggling laundry operator. The family went back to Hong Kong in 1916 and Kingman grew up there, studying

Artist **Dong Kingman** at Kilauea volcano on the island of Hawaii

painting at a local university. At the age of 18, he returned to the United States, working first in an overall factory, then in a restaurant, and finally as a houseboy, doing what painting he could in his spare time. In 1936 he was at last able to devote himself seriously to full-time painting with the help of the Works Progress Administration program, which provided work for artists during the depression years. Today Mr. Kingman not only pursues his own career as an artist but also teaches art and is in great demand as a lecturer.

One of Hollywood's most distinguished movie cameramen, James Wong Howe, was born in China and came to the United States in 1904, when his family emigrated to the state of Washington. When he was a young man, Jimmy Howe started out on a career as a professional prizefighter and was for a time the only Chinese fighter in America. But he was less than five feet tall and slightly built, and however quick and agile he learned to be, he got beaten more often than he liked. He soon retired from prizefighting and was taken on as junior assistant to a movie cameraman, mostly to lug the heavy equipment around and to set it up for the next take.

Jimmy became fascinated by the work of a cameraman. Soon he bought his own camera and experimented by taking pictures of the leading movie actresses of the day. He evolved a technique of photographing them so that they seemed even more beautiful than they really were, and he was soon in great demand. Greta Garbo is said to have insisted on him for the films in which she starred. Jimmy Howe has worked for most of the great studios, including Metro-Goldwyn-Mayer, Fox Studios, Warner Brothers, Selznick Studios, and Columbia Pictures, and has the reputation of being the highest paid cameraman in Hollywood. He has won Oscars for his photography in *The Rose Tatoo* and in *Hud*. Other well-known films of his include *Come Back Little Sheba*, *The Last Angry Man*, and *The Old Man and the Sea*.

Many other Chinese Americans have outstanding reputations in the arts. A few of the writers of Chinese ancestry are Chiang Yee, who writes travelogues and stories for children; Jade Snow Wong and Pardee Lowe, both of whom have written autobiographical books on growing up in American Chinatowns; and Lin

James Wong Howe proudly displays the Oscar awarded him in 1963 for his photography in the movie *Hud*.

Ieoh Ming Pei has designed many outstanding buildings constructed in cities throughout the United States.

Yutang, author of many best-selling books dealing with life and philosophy in China. The bass-baritone concert soloist Yi Kwei Sze is the first Chinese singer in the United States to win international fame. Wen Chung Chou was the first Chinese-American composer to win a Guggenheim Fellowship. In his compositions, he combines the classical Chinese style of music with the Western style, as Dong Kingman has done in his paintings.

Architecture is both an art and a science, and one of the most distinguished architects of recent years is a Chinese American, Ieoh Ming Pei. Pei, who was already well known for his award-winning projects in Denver, Honolulu, Pittsburgh, New York, Los Angeles, and Washington, recently won the coveted assignment of designing the John F. Kennedy Library, to be built in Cambridge, Massachusetts. (The library will be a part of a memorial to the late president.) Pei has also created a design for a standard air traffic control tower, which will be built at 25 major American airports.

Ieoh Ming Pei was born in Canton in 1917, the son of a banker. In 1935 he came to the United States to study architecture at the University of Pennsylvania but then transferred to the school of architectural engineering at the Massachusetts Institute of Technology. He was so torn between the two fields that he finally decided to take degrees in both. He graduated from MIT in 1940 and did graduate work at Harvard. After teaching at Harvard for several years, Pei established his own architectural firm, with headquarters in New York City. He became a naturalized American citizen in 1954.

5. *Research Scientists*

In 1957 two Chinese research physicists, Tsung Dao Lee and Chen Ning Yang, were awarded the Nobel Prize for their services to science in disproving the principle of the conservation of parity.

Tsung Dao Lee accepting the Nobel Prize for Physics in 1957

Working together at Columbia University, the two scientists demonstrated that the law of parity, which had governed research in nuclear physics for 30 years, did not always hold true. By making this discovery, they opened the way for important developments in the investigation of the elementary particles of the atomic nucleus.

Professors Lee and Yang were both born in China, of professional families, and both studied at universities there. In 1946 Lee won a Chinese government fellowship which gave him the opportunity to travel to the University of Chicago for advanced studies. Yang had gone to Chicago the previous year, and that is where the two scientists met. They both became students of Enrico Fermi, the physicist who helped to develop the atomic bomb.

Professor Lee took his Ph.D. from the University of Chicago in 1950 and then received a fellowship at Princeton's Institute for Advanced Study. Soon afterward he became professor of physics at Columbia University. Professor Yang took his doctorate in physics in 1948 and became a member of the Institute for Advance Study the following year. He joined the faculty at Columbia in 1953.

Both Lee and Yang were helped in their experiments on the law of the conservation of parity by Dr. Chien-Shiung Wu, professor of physics at Columbia University. She, too, was born in China, of an academic family. She graduated from the University of Nanking and came to the United States for postgraduate studies. Dr. Wu was only 27 when she was appointed to teach nuclear physics at Princeton University. Later she went to Columbia University to work on the Manhattan project, the project that was responsible for the development of the atomic bomb.

Many other Chinese people in the United States have distinguished themselves in scientific fields such as biochemistry and medical research. In the field of cancer research, Dr. Min

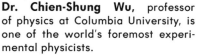

Dr. Chien-Shung Wu, professor of physics at Columbia University, is one of the world's foremost experimental physicists.

Chin Li of the Sloan-Kettering Institute caused regression of cancer with a chemical he was studying. Dr. Shin Min Chang, assistant professor of microbiology at Harvard University, developed the first man-made mutation of a human cell. Dr. C. H. Li, a biochemist at the University of California medical school in San Francisco, succeeded in isolating the hormones produced by the pituitary gland. Dr. T. H. Lee of the Bronx Veterans Administration Hospital determined the structure of ACTH, one of the most important pituitary hormones.

For centuries the Chinese have maintained a tradition of respect for intellectual studies, for fine craftsmanship, and for plain hard work. This same tradition remains strong among Americans of Chinese ancestry, whether they came to the United States as uneducated laborers or as well-educated sons and daughters of wealthy and influential families. Now that the racial barriers are coming down and opportunities can be more equally shared, Chinese Americans are putting their cultural traditions to good use.

benevolent associations, 58-59, 66
Boxer Rebellion, 21
Buck, Pearl, 79-80
Buddhism, 10, 64
Burlingame Treaty, 18, 45-46
busing, opposition of Chinese
    Americans to, 72-73

California: Chinese immigration to,
    18, 20, 28-30, 31; discovery of
    gold in, 27-28; early settlement
    of, 26-27; gold rush, 30-31, 33
Canton, 11-13, 15, 16, 17
Canton River, 20, 29
Cape Horn, 15, 28
Cape of Good Hope, 14
Central Pacific Company, 33, 34-35,
    36
Chan, Charlie, 78, 79
Chang, Shin Min, 93
Chiang Kai-shek, 22-24, 73
Chiang Mei-ling (Madame Chiang
    Kai-shek), 22, 51, 78
Chinatowns: characteristics of,
    57-58; reasons for existence of,
    56-57. See also individual cities
China Youth, 72
Chin dynasty, 8
Chinese American Citizens
    Alliance, 71
Chinese Exclusion Act (1882), 30,
    43, 46, 51
Chinese restaurants, 82
Chinese Six Companies, 29, 31, 33,
    34, 59, 66
chinoiserie, 15, 80-81
Chou dynasty, 7
Chou, Wen Chung, 90
Columbus, 11
Communist Party (Chinese), 22-24,
    73
Confucian principles, 8, 9, 22, 54
Confucius, 7-8, 9

Crocker, Charles, 34, 35, 36

Dana, Richard Henry, 26-27
depression of 1870s, 37, 39, 43,
    59, 75
Derby, Elias Hasket, 14
discrimination against Chinese
    Americans, 32, 37-38, 39-42
district associations, 58, 65

earthquake, San Francisco, 45, 59,
    62-63
East India Company, 13, 16
education of Chinese Americans,
    70, 83
Empress of China, 13-14

family associations, 58, 65
Fifteen Passenger Bill, 45
fong, 57-58
Fong, Hiram L., 85-76
Formosa. See Taiwan
Fu Manchu, 78-79

Geary Act (1892), 46
Genghis Khan, 10
ginseng, 14
Grand Turk, 14
Great Wall of China, 8

Han dynasty, 9, 10
Han Wu, 9
Hawaiian Islands, 34, 36, 49-50
Hong Kong, 17, 29, 53, 71
hong merchants, 11
hong trading system, 12-13, 17
Howe, James Wong, 88-89

Immigration Act of 1924, 49
immigration legislation, 46, 49,
    51-53, 71

Japan, attack on China of, 23

Kearney, Denis, 40, 77
Kingman, Dong, 87-88, 90

Kublai Khan, 10
Kuomingtang. *See* Nationalist Party
Kwangtung province, 20, 28-29, 53, 60

Lee, Rose Hum, 77-78
Lee, T. H., 93
Lee, Tsung Dao, 91-92
Li, C. H., 93
Li, Min Chin, 92-93
Lin Yutang, 89-90
Los Angeles, Chinatown in, 68-69, 72
Lowe, Pardee, 67, 89

Macao, 11
mah-jong, 57, 81
Manchu dynasty, 18-19, 21-22, 32-33, 64
Mandarin (language), 64-65
mandarins, 8, 9, 18, 21
Mao Tse-tung, 22, 73
Mongol Empire, 10

Nanking Treaty, 17
Nationalist Party (Chinese), 22-24, 53, 76
New Year, Chinese, 58, 61, 66
New York City, Chinatown in, 69-70, 72
Nixon, Richard M., 24-25

occupations of Chinese Americans, 83
Ong, Wing F., 86
opium trade, 15-16, 17
Opium War, 16-17

Pacific Railway Bill, 33
paper sons, 49
Pei, Ieoh Ming, 90-91
Polo, Marco, 10
population, Chinese American, distribution of, 68

quota system, 51, 52, 53
queues, 32-33, 44, 64

railroad, transcontinental, 33-36
Red Guard, 72
religion of Chinese Americans, 64

Sacramento, Cal., 33, 34
San Francisco: Chinatown in, 56, 59-67, 72; discrimination against Chinese in, 44-45; early settlement of, 26-27; earthquake in, 48, 62-63; during gold rush, 28, 29, 31
Scott Act (1888), 46
Shang dynasty, 7
Shanghai, 17, 21, 23, 24
Shih Huang Ti, 8, 9
Shoong, Joe, 86
Sierra Nevada, 34, 35
Six Companies. *See* Chinese Six Companies
smuggling of Chinese immigrants, 47
Sun Yat-sen, 22
Sutter, John, 27, 28

Taiping revolt, 19-20
Taiwan, 24, 53
Toishan, 20, 66
tongs, 61, 65-66
Tsai, Gerald, Jr., 87
Tung, C. Y., 87
Twain, Mark, 42

Union Pacific Company, 33, 36

Whampoa Island, 11
women, traditional role of, in Chinatown, 60-61, 71
Wong, Anna May, 79
Wong, Jade Snow, 67, 89
Workingman's Party, 40, 75, 77
Wu, Chien-Shiung, 92

Yang, Chen Ning, 91-92
Yee, Chiang, 89

The IN AMERICA *Series*

The AMERICAN INDIAN *in America, Volume I*
The AMERICAN INDIAN *in America, Volume II*
The CHINESE *in America*
The CZECHS & SLOVAKS *in America*
The DUTCH *in America*
The EAST INDIANS & PAKISTANIS *in America*
The ENGLISH *in America*
The FRENCH *in America*
The GERMANS *in America*
The GREEKS *in America*
The HUNGARIANS *in America*
The IRISH *in America*
The ITALIANS *in America*
The JAPANESE *in America*
The JEWS *in America*
The MEXICANS *in America*
The NEGRO *in America*
The NORWEGIANS *in America*
The POLES *in America*
The PUERTO RICANS *in America*
The RUSSIANS *in America*
The SCOTS & SCOTCH-IRISH *in America*
The SWEDES *in America*
The UKRAINIANS *in America*
The FREEDOM OF THE PRESS *in America*
The FREEDOM OF RELIGION *in America*
The FREEDOM OF SPEECH *in America*

We specialize in publishing quality books for
young people. For a complete list please write:

 Lerner Publications Company
241 First Avenue North, Minneapolis, Minnesota 55401